ORCAS EVERYWHERE

The Mystery and History of Killer Whales

MARK LEIREN-YOUNG

ORCA BOOK PUBLISHERS

Library and Archives Canada Cataloguing in Publication
Title: Orcas everywhere: the mystery and history of killer whales / Mark Leiren-Young.
Names: Leiren-Young, Mark, author.

Description: Series statement: Orca wild | Includes bibliographical references and index.

Identifiers: Canadiana (print) 20190068825 | Canadiana (ebook) 20190068949 | ISBN 9781459819986
(hardcover) | ISBN 9781459820005 (PDF) | ISBN 9781459819993 (EPUB)

Subjects: LCSH: Killer whale—Juvenile literature./LCSH: Killer whale—History—Juvenile literature.

Classification: LCC QL737.C432 L45 2019 | DDC j599.53 | 6–dc23

Library of Congress Control Number: 2019934044
Simultaneously published in Canada and the United States in 2019

Summary: Launching the new Orca Wild series, this nonfiction book for middle readers takes a deep dive into the lives of orcas
(also known as killer whales). Illustrated with archival and contemporary photographs.

*Orca Book Publishers is committed to reducing the consumption of nonrenewable resources in the making of our books.
We make every effort to use materials that support a sustainable future.*

Orca Book Publishers gratefully acknowledges the support for its publishing programs provided by
the following agencies: the Government of Canada, the Canada Council for the Arts and the Province
of British Columbia through the BC Arts Council and the Book Publishing Tax Credit.

Front cover photo by Pascal Kobeh/naturepl.com
Back cover photo by Clint Rivers
Author photo by Mark Halliday

Edited by Sarah N. Harvey
Design by Jenn Playford

ORCA BOOK PUBLISHERS
orcabook.com

Printed and bound in China.

22 21 20 19 • 4 3 2 1

Orcas on the move in Norway.
KRISZTINA BALOTAY

For Rayne, the whale whisperer, and for everyone
doing what they can to save the orcas, oceans and
environment. Since you're reading this book,
I hope that includes you.

CONTENTS

"Orca culture is complex, sophisticated, and if scientists saw anything like this on another planet they'd declare we'd found intelligent life."

—from the documentary film
The Hundred-Year-Old Whale

INTRODUCTION
The Splash Zone

Mark Leiren-Young at the Whale Museum in Friday Harbor, WA.
RAYNE ELLYCRYS BENU

When I was making a movie about orcas, I asked everyone I interviewed to tell me about the first time they saw a whale. People smiled as they conjured their memories. Big smiles. The word that kept coming up from everyone—no matter how young or old—was *magical*.

Whales, especially killer whales, don't just fascinate us; they enchant us.

The first time I saw a whale, she was in a tank at the Vancouver Aquarium.

Skana was four years old. I was five.

At just under 15 feet long (4.5 meters) and weighing about 3,000 pounds (1,361 kilograms), Skana was the biggest animal I'd ever seen. As she leaped and dove and raced at her trainer's commands, it was clear she was smart—very smart. And seeing her up close rocked my world.

If you sat in the rows closest to her pool, Skana would spray you with water. If you were lucky, when she leaped and landed you'd get soaked. This was the "splash zone." This was where every kid wanted to be. Yes, it was magical.

Skana arrived at the Vancouver Aquarium in 1967. She was given the Haida name for killer whale—*Skaana*. This was translated at the time as "killer demon" or "supernatural power." Back then people knew so little about whales that when she showed up her name was Walter, since experts were sure she was a he. Skana was one of only five captive orcas in the world.

Skana on display at the Vancouver Aquarium. COURTESY OF TERRY MCLEOD

Skana with trainer Terry McLeod at the Vancouver Aquarium.
COURTESY OF TERRY McLEOD

When Skana moved to the aquarium it seemed everyone in Vancouver—everyone everywhere—wanted to meet her. Canada's then prime minister, Pierre Trudeau, held a fish to feed Skana and grinned like a kid as she snatched it from him.

Yes, the prime minister stood in the splash zone.

In 1968 Skana was joined by a baby male orca named Hyak.

As I got older Skana's pool started looking smaller to me.

Over the years Skana's pool started looking smaller to almost everyone.

As an adult I wrote about whether it was time to stop keeping whales in pools and learned about Moby Doll. Moby was caught by the Vancouver Aquarium a few years before "Walter" showed up. He was the first orca to survive for more than two days in captivity. While I was studying Moby I learned more about Skana. Once again, more than over thirty years after her death, she rocked my world.

Paul Spong, a neuroscientist from New Zealand who was studying Skana and Hyak, was sure orcas were intelligent, had a sense of humor and shouldn't be kept in captivity or killed in the wild.

Skana at the Vancouver Aquarium.
COURTESY OF TERRY McLEOD

Back then many countries hunted whales for oil, fertilizer and food—sometimes for pet food. But to stop the whaling industry, Spong needed help.

In 1971 a few dozen people in Vancouver got together to protest nuclear testing in the United States. The American military was setting off atomic bombs in Alaska to study what happened. The protesters called themselves "Greenpeace."

Spong hoped to get Greenpeace to take on a new cause. He invited Bob Hunter, one of the Greenpeace leaders,

The first Greenpeace mission to save the whales. REX WEYLER/GREENPEACE

to the aquarium. Spong asked Hunter to do a "trick" with Skana. He wanted the media to have a perfect photo to promote Greenpeace's new campaign to save the whales.

People who worked with Skana sometimes put their head in her mouth to prove how gentle she was, how much they trusted her. Spong had done this. Many of Skana's trainers did this. Hunter wasn't keen on sticking his neck out, but finally, reluctantly, he agreed.

As Skana closed her mouth, just enough to let Hunter feel the tips of her teeth, she rocked his world. Hunter and Spong shifted Greenpeace's focus from fighting against nuclear testing to fighting for whales.

I've heard people call the first orcas in aquariums martyrs, prisoners, entertainers and ambassadors. Skana, the ambassador from Planet Orca, helped inspire the fight to save all whales everywhere. Spong often told people that Greenpeace worked for Skana.

Spong also told people, including me, that if Skana and her family were called "killer whales," we should be called "killer apes." Spong always refers to Skana, Hyak and all their relatives as "orcas."

This book is an introduction to the "orcaverse." I hope it will help you fall in love with these whales like I have and do what you can to respect, protect and revive their habitat.

Now picture an orca like Skana checking you out with a curious eye bigger than your head, wondering what you are, who you are, and letting loose a squeal to say hello.

Pretend you're at home with her in the ocean, in the true splash zone.

ORCA BITES

Hello, Skana!

Skana was caught off the coast of Washington State in 1967. The six-year-old southern resident orca was originally displayed in a tiny tank at the Vancouver Boat, Trailer and Sport Show. Skana's captors thought she was a boy and named her Walter. Over 100,000 people turned up to see the captive orca. At the show, Walter was part of the world's first whale-to-whale phone call. Ted Griffin, one of the men who'd caught her, put her on the line to chat with captive orcas in Seattle. The call was broadcast on the radio and guaranteed that Walter was a local star. The Vancouver Aquarium bought the whale for $20,000. She quickly became one of Vancouver's most famous citizens and one of Canada's top tourist attractions.

Scarlet and Slick in the Salish Sea.
TASLI SHAW

1

Queen of the Salish Sea

"The value of having old whales is that they know the whole system and they lead the others and they babysit."

—Ken Balcomb, founder, Center for Whale Research

Spy-hopping

One way orcas (and other marine animals) can see what's going on above the surface is to "hop" up and spy what's happening. This allows them to get a clear view of the surface world and for the "podparazzi" to get clear shots of the orcas.

Ocean Sun pops her head above the wild waves to greet the dawn. At 20 feet (6 meters) long and 7,000 pounds (3,175 kilograms), this orca looks like she's standing on the tip of her hefty tail. She's *spy-hopping*—balancing straight up in the water—so her huge eyes spy what's above the surface of the ocean her family calls home.

The white marks on her slick, rubbery, black-and-white skin look like they were added by someone drawing a whale warrior queen. White stripes accent both eyes. Behind the big fin on her back—the *dorsal*—is a pattern found on all orcas, known as a *saddle patch*. Each saddle patch is unique, like a giant fingerprint. Ocean Sun's pattern looks like an unfinished valentine or perhaps a broken heart.

Ocean Sun turns to the younger whales in her family. And since she's almost a century old, all the other orcas are younger than her. The senior whale shares what she's seeing with squeaks, squeals and a super sense you and I don't have and can only imagine—*sonar*.

Orcas create and share pictures of everything around them by sending out sounds—like bats do. This method of scanning the world is called *biosonar*—a personal sonar system that uses *echolocation*. Orcas (and bats) send out sounds and register how they bounce off whatever is in front of them. For now we'll call those sounds *pings*.

Pings from other orcas add more information.

Because they share this sense, the more orcas sending Pings, the clearer the undersea world becomes to all of them.

Ping.

The orcas know the shape of the Chinook salmon.

Ping.

The orcas know the size of their prey.

Chinook salmon proving why we also call them kings. EVAL LINELL/ SHUTTERSTOCK.COM

Ping.

The salmon turns. And the orcas know which way the panicked fish is racing.

Ping.

The chase is on…

And because orcas can travel at over 30 miles (50 kilometers) an hour and salmon swim less than 2 miles (3 kilometers) an hour, the chase doesn't last long.

Orcas see as well as we do, but they hear things we can't. They know what's coming from up to 30 miles (48 kilometers) away, and they share this information using their songs, squeals and splashes. So Ocean Sun knows something special is happening.

PODCASTING

Ocean Sun is the queen of the *Salish Sea*, but she doesn't get a throne, a crown, a scepter or her own Disney movie. If she's lucky, the elder orca gets clean, clear, quiet water to swim in and plenty of salmon to snack on.

Humans like to stay put in neighborhoods, but orcas take friends and family with them. Their communities are called *pods*. And orca pods everywhere have their own sets of calls called *dialects*.

Orcas in the Pacific Ocean don't sound the same as orcas in any other ocean. But even pods who share the same stretch of sea have completely distinct dialects.

When I first learned this term from Dr. John Ford, the Canadian scientist who discovered orca dialects, I assumed they were like accents. I imagined orcas who sounded Canadian, American, Australian or British. Ford explained that they are as distinctive as English, Japanese and Swahili. There's more about orca languages in chapter 10.

Ocean Sun belongs to a group of orcas known as *southern residents*, who live in the Salish Sea.

A *resident* is someone who lives somewhere on a long-term basis. Your home is your residence. You are a resident of your home.

The southern residents' residence is the ocean off the coast of southern British Columbia. Michael Bigg, the scientist who tagged the orcas "southern," was Canadian. The orcas he called "transients"—because they don't stay put—are now known as *Bigg's whales*.

Southern residents were the first orcas caught, displayed and studied by humans. The most famous orcas in the world, the southern residents have likely been photographed more often than Britain's royal family. Every day they are followed by hundreds, sometimes thousands, of what I call "podparazzi."

A Bigg's orca (T46B2) swimming with her supper in the Salish Sea.
VAL SHORE

Slick from J pod spy-hopping to see what's happening above the water.
NATIONAL OCEANIC AND ATMOSPHERIC ADMINISTRATION/DEPARTMENT OF COMMERCE

Ocean Sun and her clan eat only sushi. Well, sort of. They feed on fresh raw fish, but they don't need seaweed, rice, ginger, wasabi or chopsticks. They also won't look at much else on the menu. Yes, there are plenty of fish in the sea, but not for resident orcas.

The southern residents like only one type of salmon—Chinook (also known as king). So when there are a lot of Chinook, southern residents eat well. When there aren't, it's very hard to be a southern resident.

Orcas all over the world are *matriarchal*. This means the females are in charge. The boss—or matriarch—is the oldest female. So in orca society, the oldest females, like Ocean Sun, lead because they know the secrets of the seas.

WHO OR WHAT IS AN ORCA?

In most books about animals, an orca like Ocean Sun would be called a *what*, not a *who*, an *it,* not a *she.*

Bigg's orcas navigating the Salish Sea.
CLINT RIVERS

Historically, anything nonhuman is grammatically—and philosophically—considered a thing, an object.

Grammar sets out the rules of a language. It helps us know how we should use capital letters, commas and question marks.

Philosophy sets out the rules for being human. It tells us how we should treat one another.

When I wrote my book *The Killer Whale Who Changed the World*, the original title was *The Killer Whale That Changed the World*.

Grammatically, *that* is the correct pronoun to use for a whale. Philosophically it felt wrong to me. I didn't believe the orca I was writing about—Moby Doll—was an "it."

Today, using the same language for animals as we use for people is rare. I don't think it will be for much longer. But until that changes, if you write or talk about orcas the way I do, and someone challenges you on your grammar, maybe you can challenge them on their philosophy.

Harbor seals—or, as Bigg's whales like to call them, lunch—lounging on the rocks in the Salish Sea.
RAYNE ELLYCRYS BENU

2

Moms and Matriarchs

"The orca, like any other
species, does not exist alone.
It requires an entire web
of life to sustain its presence."

—Alexandra Morton,
Listening to Whales: What the Orcas Have Taught Us

Apex predator

Apex means "top." A predator is any animal that eats another. The animal being hunted and eaten is *prey*—which is the word we use to describe the diet of animals that eat others. Orcas are fussy eaters, but they could eat whatever they want. No animal in the water eats them, so they're the apex predator. There are apex predators in the ocean, on land and in the air.

OCEAN SUN

Researchers have estimated that Ocean Sun was born in 1928, and she hasn't told anyone otherwise. Scientists weren't paying much attention to orcas until the 1970s, so her probable birthday was based on her family relationships and the last time humans know she gave birth.

So let's imagine Ocean Sun's world when she was born, in 1928.

Humans didn't have computers or TVs. Telephones were still so new that we'd just made the first call to someone across an ocean. Movies came in the same colors as orcas (black and white). Electricity was a luxury. So we didn't know much about technology or whales.

When Ocean Sun was born, humans weren't dumping as many poisons into the water or polluting the air by driving cars (since most people couldn't afford this expensive new invention). And pretty much nothing was made of plastic.

Not only were there almost no airplanes, but not many people used boats or trains either.

And there weren't that many of us yet. In 1928 there were only two billion humans on the globe. So orcas didn't encounter much pollution or many people. Today there are almost eight billion of us. People and pollution are everywhere.

Back then most humans called Ocean Sun's species "killer whales," since different types of orcas eat all sorts of animals. But because humans tend to think the world revolves around us, we assumed that killer whales got their name because they kill people.

Because orcas are the ocean's *apex predator* they are the heavyweight champions of the seas. There are bigger fish—

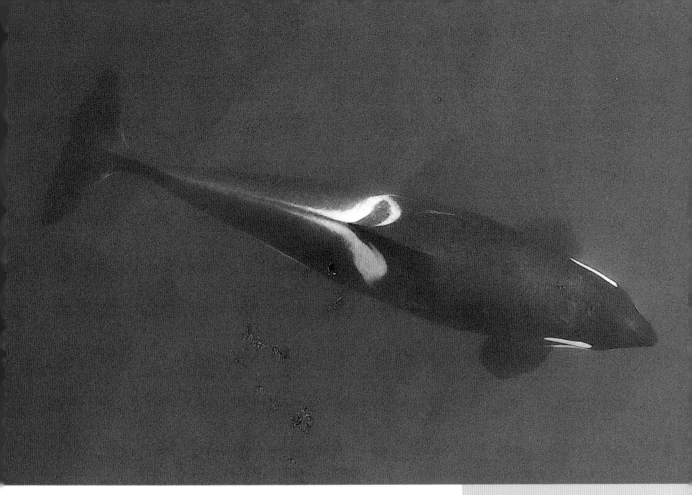

Aerial image of Ocean Sun from a flying drone 100 feet (30 meters) above the whale. JOHN DURBAN (NOAA), HOLLY FEARNBACH (SR3) AND LANCE BARRETT-LENNARD (CORI)

and mammals—but for hundreds of thousands of years, perhaps since the beginning of time, the only animals who have ever been a threat to orcas are humans.

Since orcas eat other animals (including fish, whales, dolphins, manta rays, sea lions, sea birds, sea turtles, seals, squid and even great white sharks), most humans assumed they'd happily snack on us.

We didn't know that orcas don't consider people a proper part of a balanced diet.

So orcas like Ocean Sun had no way of knowing why soldiers were shooting at her pod for target practice.

Orca chow

Orcas have snacked on at least 31 other types of cetaceans, 19 kinds of seals and sea lions, 44 bony fish, 22 sharks and rays, 20 birds, 5 squid and octopuses, 1 sea turtle, a moose and a horse. There are suspicions that Bigg's orcas have also dined on deer.

Fishermen carried rifles to kill her family because they didn't want to share "their" salmon. Also, the dreaded killers scared tourists. In 1960 the Canadian government mounted a machine gun on the shore of Vancouver Island to combat the orca menace.

Thankfully, that gun was never fired.

Now Ocean Sun is taking her clan to meet the two other pods of southern residents. When pods get together their gathering is called a *superpod*. Today Ocean Sun will be the oldest orca in attendance. She became the southern residents' matriarch in 2016, after the death of an orca known as Granny.

GRANNY

When I was making a movie about Granny, some researchers estimated she was born in 1911. When we set out to film her, she would have been 104.

The orca Granny breaching at the end of a long day. CLINT RIVERS

The challenge in determining an orca's age is that there is no definitive way to do it. With trees, you can cut them down and count the rings to see how many years they've lived. There isn't a corresponding method with orcas, so scientists use whatever facts they have to determine the age of orcas born before we started studying them.

Granny's age was estimated on the basis of her relationship with her pod and her apparent age when she was caught and released in the early 1970s. Researchers also knew she had not given birth since she was set free.

We know orcas mature at about the same rate as we do, and since humans can live to over 100, there's no reason orcas can't. Marine mammals—and other sea life like sharks—live much longer in arctic temperatures. Even if Granny was 105 when she died, she wasn't the oldest whale in the world. Bowhead whales up north can live over 200 years. People have found harpoon tips in their blubber that confirm their ages. Sharks in icy northern waters can live over 400 years.

But Granny lived and died in the very toxic Salish Sea.

It would be surprising if orcas don't live longer in areas that are less polluted by poisons and plastics. Orcas in the Salish Sea are exposed to so much pollution that some dead whales are treated like they're radioactive. The people who deal with their bodies have to wear special protective suits to avoid exposure to toxic chemicals. So it's likely our estimates for how long orcas can live are based on some of the world's shortest-lived orcas.

If an orca full of poisons can live for a century, how long can an orca live in a relatively unpolluted area with a healthy food supply?

ORCA BITES

The grandmother hypothesis

There are only three species on earth whose females live for a long time after they can no longer give birth—humans, orcas and pilot whales. A new study shows that belugas, narwhals and false killer whales may share this trait. The idea of an animal living after it's too old to reproduce seemed to defy the logic of evolution. Scientists wondered why this happened. This led to a theory that explains why orcas like Ocean Sun live so many years after they can no longer have babies. The theory—the grandmother hypothesis—is that in a complex society, knowledge matters more than reproduction. Grandmothers are needed to share their wisdom.

Connection, by Andy Everson, shows an orca swimming in the waters beneath the Comox Glacier in BC.

3

Wolves of the Sea

"In whatever quarter of the world [killer whales] are found, they seem always intent upon seeking something to destroy or devour."

—American naturalist Captain Charles Scammon, 1874

ORCA BITES

What's a mammal?

Scientists are keen on classifying things. Humans are classified as mammals. So are orcas and apes and cows and elephants. Most mammals share all sorts of traits, but the key to deciding who belongs to Team Mammal is if moms produce milk to feed their babies from mammary glands (which is where we get the word *mammal*). The platypus is a mammal that sweats milk, but the platypus seems to exist just to confuse scientists.

Orcas used to scare the heck out of us. And if you've ever seen an orca eat whales, seals or sea lions, it's easy to understand why.

When I give talks about orcas, I'll often ask if anyone can imagine being afraid of one. Almost everyone laughs, because they're picturing an orca like Ocean Sun. Most people interested in orcas know they're friendly, intelligent and lovable.

But one night when I was talking about orcas on Salt Spring Island—a small island in the Salish Sea—most people *could* imagine being scared of an orca. A few years earlier a pod of Bigg's whales beached a minke (a small whale, but bigger than most orcas). Over the next few hours the orcas tore their catch to shreds on the rocks of the island's shore.

One teenager tried to save the doomed minke by throwing stones at the orcas.

Some people cheered as the orcas attacked and ate the minke.

Some people cried as the minke became a meal.

Those people had no trouble picturing orcas as killers.

I once watched a Bigg's whale chase a terrified seal who escaped certain doom by jumping onto the back of a whale-watching boat. The tourists were delighted. The orcas, who kept circling the boat and eying that terrified seal, were not.

One nickname for orcas that is used around the world is "wolves of the sea," because orcas hunt in packs like wolves do. And also like wolves, they take down prey much larger than themselves. Orcas will separate a young or weak whale from its pod, chase this prey until it's exhausted and then move in for the kill.

The Nuu-chah-nulth and Makah people who live near the Salish Sea say orcas can turn into wolves and walk around the land. The Yupik in Siberia say orcas used to be wolves.

I have friends who saw a Bigg's whale use his mighty tail to toss a terrified seal about 80 feet (24 meters) into the air. This type of seemingly cruel behavior is probably meant to teach babies how to hunt or make it easier to remove the skin so orcas don't swallow fur. But it is how orcas developed a reputation for being as brutal as humans. Many people thought orcas were the only species besides humans who hunted for fun.

Someone asked me whether a killer whale could take down a megalodon—the biggest shark that ever lived. My answer: "I'd put my money on the pod (assuming we're talking about mammal-eating orcas) because orcas have no trouble taking on great white sharks. The megalodon has the size and the teeth, but the orcas have the brains. I'll bet on brains."

If you've seen mammal-eating orcas hunt, fearing them seems like the right response. They didn't get the name killer whale just because it sounded cool. A pair of African orcas has become infamous for killing great white sharks. The duo flips them over (so they can't swim away) and feasts on their organs.

If you're on an orca's grocery list, you won't last long.

A scared seal hiding out from Bigg's orcas in the Salish Sea. MARK LEIREN-YOUNG

WHY DON'T KILLER WHALES KILL US?

Why aren't humans on an orca's menu? That's what everyone wants to know.

Dr. Lance Barrett-Lennard has studied orcas since 1984. The Canadian scientist told me orcas eat only what Mom teaches them to eat. So if Mom doesn't snack on humans—or squid for that matter—neither will her calves.

One reason for this might be that if an orca eats something that doesn't go down properly, it would be easy to choke. And we're pretty bony. Orcas also know exactly what they're eating.

Even on the rare occasions that sharks take a bite out of a person (and this happens less than 100 times a year), they almost always spit us out and move on. In 2017 eighty-eight shark attacks were reported around the world. Only five of the humans were killed. As Rob Stewart pointed out in his movie *Sharkwater Extinction*, falling soda machines kill more people each year than sharks do. Repeat after me: sharks don't eat us. But because sharks tend to use sight and smells to find food, a human could be mistaken for a seal or sea lion.

A great white shark that was attacked by orcas. COURTESY OF CARI ROETS

Orcas rely on echolocation and pretty much look inside their prey. So even if you stepped into the water wearing a seal suit smeared with fresh salmon guts, they still wouldn't snack on a crunchy, bland human.

Or maybe orcas are just nicer than we are.

Imagine if an alien species shot us, kidnapped our children and chased us when we tried to eat or nap. How long do you think it would be before humans declared war?

Whether they're trapped in tanks or swimming free, orcas don't just tolerate humans—they're almost always nice to us. Some scientists say this could prove that being nice is an evolutionary advantage, which would mean orcas are more evolved than we are. Since they've been around 10 million years longer than we have, that would make sense.

I suspect scientists prefer to credit evolution rather than attitude, as otherwise they'd have to consider the possibility that orcas might be more humane than humans.

Canadian filmmaker Rob Stewart swimming
with the sharks.
SHARKWATER PRODUCTIONS

Tsuchi (J31), Comet (K038) and Deadhead
(K27) swim by Seattle in the wintertime.
CANDICE EMMONS/NATIONAL OCEANIC AND
ATMOSPHERIC ADMINISTRATION/DEPARTMENT
OF COMMERCE

4

Right Whales and Wrong Whales

"And God created great whales, and every living creature that moveth, which the waters brought forth abundantly, after their kind, and every winged fowl after his kind: and God saw that it was good."

—Genesis 1:21 (King James Version)

A baleen whale showing off the baleen!
CLINT RIVERS

Baleen

Baleen is a strainer system made of *keratin* (the same protein human hair and finger nails are made of) that whales use to eat zooplankton. Baleen was once used the same way we later used plastic because it was strong and flexible. This is also the name used for all whales who have baleen instead of teeth.

Orcas evolved in our oceans about 11 million years ago. That's more than 10 million years before *Homo sapiens* (that's us) arrived. Christian, Jewish and Muslim holy books agree that whales got here first.

Humans have hunted whales since prehistoric times. But in about 1000 CE humans became really good at killing whales.

Commercial whaling started when fishermen from the Basque Country in southern Europe wiped out almost all the North Atlantic right whales. Adult right whales weigh up to 100 tons (91 tonnes), can grow up to 65 feet (20 meters) long and are full of oil.

They are also the biggest *baleen* whales. These whales don't have teeth; they have baleen (which whalers called *whalebone*) that strains out almost everything in the water except the *zooplankton* these whales find so tasty.

Commercial whaling became *industrial whaling* in the 1870s after Norwegian Svend Foyn invented a harpoon gun. Hunters in fast boats would chase and catch whales with the new harpoon. Men on floating factory ships butchered the whales and drained their oil.

Today right whales are one of the rarest whales, despite being one of the first species declared off-limits by the League of Nations in 1931. That year at least 43,000 whales were killed commercially.

In 1949 the International Convention for the Regulation of Whaling also declared right whales off-limits, but countries were supposed to police themselves. Whaling was regulated because whales were considered one of the world's most important resources.

Until the 1960s, whale bones, teeth, flesh and oil were used to make things like perfume, pet food, candles, soap and carvings. Whale oil was used to light lamps and make machines run smoothly. Whale parts were used then the way plastic is now.

Whichever whale was the right one, orcas were wrong. The Japanese and Norwegians caught some orcas (for food), but almost no one else did. In North America, fishermen were either scared of them or annoyed by them and carried rifles to shoot at "pests" they called blackfish and other names.

Anyone who has spent time near the waters orcas inhabit knows these mammals are intelligent. That also means they're trouble—at least for fishermen.

The Russian whale hunt in the 1970s.
REX WEYLER/GREENPEACE

They're tough to kill, and they eat the same fish we do. Orcas regularly snatch fish from fishermen in places like Alaska and the Strait of Gibraltar. Fishermen have traditionally responded by killing orcas.

In 1954 the government of Iceland asked the US navy to kill orcas to protect the herring. *Time* magazine reported on one of the missions to slaughter what they called "savage sea cannibals." The navy used rifles and machine guns to exterminate more than 100 orcas.

The next year the US navy used rockets to attack the whales.

Why did they call them cannibals?

Because the people shooting the orcas thought that when the whales raced toward their bleeding family members, they wanted to eat them. They didn't realize these orcas were prepared to die trying to save their podmates.

Whale meat for sale in Japan in the twenty-first century.
FAEROUT/ DREAMSTIME.COM

WORKING WITH WHALES

Orcas and humans used to hunt together. Following the fins of fish-eating orcas was a good way to figure out where to set fishing nets.

In Russia's Far East, orcas worked with the Kamchadals, the local Indigenous people, to herd baleen whales for human whalers.

In Australia the Indigenous Koori hunted with orcas for thousands of years. Then white settlers took over whaling and drafted the Koori—and the orcas—to assist.

From the mid-nineteenth century to the early twentieth century, three pods of orcas near New South Wales, Australia, herded baleens for whalers. The orcas alerted their human partners with splashes after they'd caught their prey. The whalers believed the pod was led by a male they named Old Tom. Since orcas are matriarchal, the pod was likely led by a female called Stranger.

The whalers of Eden, Australia, hunting together with Old Tom.
EDEN WHALING MUSEUM

The fishermen took the baleens, but not until they'd given the orcas their favorite parts of the big whales—lips and tongues. This deal was known as "the law of the tongue."

This partnership lasted until a greedy human refused to share his catch and ripped it away from Tom. Tom lost some teeth in the struggle. The injury led to his death. Tom's skeleton is still displayed in Australia's Eden Whaling Museum.

BLACK AND WHITE

Orca cultures shift around the world, but their color schemes...not so much.

Some scientists think orcas are black and white because that coloring makes it harder for prey to spot them. Another theory is that the blend of black and white makes orcas look smaller and less dangerous.

Albino is the term for animals (and humans) born with little or no *melanin*—the substance that adds color to skin, hair and eyes. Albinism for most animal species that don't live in snowy places is likely to lead to an early death. It's hard to hide in the forest or the ocean if you're all white. Even if you're the apex predator, it's harder to hunt if your prey can see you coming.

Because this condition makes it easy for humans to spot them, albino orcas often become local legends.

In the 1940s scientists on the west coast of Canada and the United States were fascinated by an albino orca they named Alice. Since no one had figured out how to identify individual orcas, Alice's coloring made it possible to study her. In the 1970s Sealand of the Pacific in Victoria, BC, caught and displayed an albino orca they called Chimo. In 2018 there were at least four (maybe as many as eight) albino orcas roaming the seas near Russia, all from different pods.

How far and how fast can whales swim?

The whales we've watched most—southern residents—swim about 75 miles (120 kilometers) each day. They usually swim about 9 miles (13 kilometers) per hour but can reach speeds of nearly 31 miles (50 kilometers) per hour if they want to.

Chimo the white whale and Haida making a splash at Sealand in Victoria, BC, in 1972. JOHN COLBY

Whale hunters harpooning a whale.
WHITEMAY/ISTOCK.COM

5

Catching a Killer

"However big the whale
may be, the tiny harpoon
can rob him of life."

—Malawi wisdom

A model of a modern harpoon from the Whaling Museum in Sandefjord, Norway. MARK LEIREN-YOUNG

The Makah on the beach after a whale hunt in 1910. ASAHEL CURTIS/SEATTLE PUBLIC LIBRARY

During the reign of Claudius Caesar (41–54 CE), Romans cornered a killer whale in Ostia harbor just outside Rome. They treated the whale the same way they treated lions. They used it for entertainment before they slaughtered it. Historian Pliny the Elder wrote that "Caesar ordered a great number of nets to be extended at the mouth of the harbor, from shore to shore… and so afforded a spectacle to the Roman people; for boats assailed the monster, while the soldiers on board showered lances upon it."

Pliny wasn't upset about this. He warned readers: "A Killer Whale cannot be properly depicted or described except as an enormous mass of flesh armed with savage teeth."

In 1759 a 24-foot (7.3-meter) orca swam into London's River Thames. The whale was caught, killed and taken to the Westminster Bridge for display. Thirteen years later an 18-foot (5.5-meter) orca was caught and killed in the Thames. In 1791 an orca reported to be 30 feet (9 meters) long was chased up the legendary British river and killed.

In the 1860s a researcher in France experimented with poisons and explosives to figure out the best ways to hunt whales. He tested bombs on a variety of whales, including several orcas.

In the nineteenth century showman P.T. Barnum was obsessed with larger-than-life exhibits. His most sizeable star was Jumbo, an elephant whose name became a new word for *really big*. So it was no surprise that he wanted a whale for his museum in New York. Even Barnum wasn't crazy enough to chase a killer whale. There was a beluga on display in Boston, so he set his sights on showing two belugas. When his hunters caught a pair of belugas in the St. Lawrence River, he put them in a tank in Boston. Then he took them to his famous New York museum.

Unfortunately, his tank was full of polluted water from New York Bay, and his new stars died in less than forty-eight hours. Another pair of belugas died en route to New York. When he finally had belugas behind glass in New York, Barnum's museum caught fire. In an attempt to put out the blaze, someone broke the glass to let out the water and the belugas died in the fire.

ORCAS AS ENTERTAINERS

The first major exhibit focusing on sea life opened in 1938 in Florida. Marine Studios (later known as Marineland of Florida) was built as a home for dolphins who would star in movies and TV shows. But the owners soon discovered that people were happy to pay to meet the undersea celebrities. The modern idea of *cetaceans* as tourist attractions was born.

In 1954 a second Marineland opened in Los Angeles. The owners of the new aquarium wanted a big star, so they set out to catch a whale. In 1957 their collectors—Frank Brocato and his godson, Frank Calandrino—equipped their fishing boat with a lasso and caught a pilot whale. Pilots are close relatives of orcas. The whale was named Bubbles, and she became Hollywood's biggest star—or at least Hollywood's largest star.

While Bubbles was a hit, the two Franks knew that everyone really wanted to see the fiercest animal on earth— the dreaded killer whale. In November 1961 an orca was

ORCA BITES

Sprouter

When a male orca is around 15 years old, he goes through a growth spurt. Orcas can likely spot what's going on with their teenage boys in all sorts of ways. Humans know what's happening because the dorsal grows or sprouts.

seen swimming alone in California's Newport Harbor. The Franks were determined to catch her.

More than 5,000 people watched the hunt from shore, cheering whenever the whale dodged the lassos and when one of the Franks fell into the water. Instead of trying to escape the harbor, the orca finally surrendered. That should have been a clue that something was wrong.

The triumphant hunters put the whale they'd named Wanda onto a raft. Then they moved the 17-foot (5-meter) orca onto a flatbed truck and covered her with wet blankets. She was driven to Marineland and transferred to a tank just a bit bigger than a two-car garage.

Marineland was having a fantastic week. A few days earlier the prime minister of India had visited and fed Bubbles. Now the aquarium's collectors had caught what he called the most vicious animal on land or sea.

Wanda refused to eat and smashed her body against her tank's walls until she died. After she died it became clear that she had been a very sick whale. Her health problems included pneumonia. Being chased around the harbor and dumped into a fish tank was more than she could take. When researchers were done studying her, Wanda's remains were taken to the dump. As a final indignity, the truck she was in stalled en route, and gawkers gathered to see her body.

The Franks decided to go killer-whale hunting again. This time they wanted to land a healthy whale, ideally a baby who could be trained to do tricks.

The first time they spotted a baby orca they roped it with their lasso. When other members of the pod lined up in what looked to the hunters like military formation, the Franks didn't want to risk a whale war. They let their orca go.

Short-finned pilot whales spy-hopping in the waters off Guam.
ADAM Ü/NATIONAL OCEANIC AND ATMOSPHERIC ADMINISTRATION/DEPARTMENT OF COMMERCE

Killer whales lining up in Alaska. Does this look like a military formation?
KIM PARSONS/NATIONAL OCEANIC AND ATMOSPHERIC ADMINISTRATION/DEPARTMENT OF COMMERCE

Orcas captured at Penn Cove in 1971.
WASHINGTON STATE ARCHIVES

In the summer of 1962 they took their boat to the Salish Sea and set up off Point Roberts, Washington. They didn't just bring gear for hunting a whale; they packed guns in case they had to battle an orca army.

The orcas seemed to know about their would-be hunters, because no pods came near them for over two months. On September 16, 1962, the capture crew spotted a female orca chasing a porpoise and lassoed the distracted predator. In the same way that seals and sea lions slide onto boats to avoid becoming lunch, the porpoise used the hunting boat to evade the orca.

The trapped orca followed the porpoise, wrapping the lasso around the propeller. She surfaced about 200 feet (61 meters) from the boat and, according to the Franks, let loose "shrill shrieks." Then a "bull orca" joined her in racing toward their boat, "striking it with their flanks." Since the whales never told their side of the story, we'll never know if they hit the boat on purpose, were chasing the porpoise or were trying to escape the lasso.

What we do know is that the Franks had already proven they were at least as scared of orcas as the poor porpoise was. But unlike the porpoise, Frank Brocato had a gun. He fired ten shots at the female and one at the male. The male escaped, but the hunters took the female's body to shore, where her body was ground up into dog food. Her teeth were taken as trophies by the hunters. The Franks were done chasing these deadly beasts.

ORCA BITES

What's a cetacean?

Cetacean is the scientific term used for all types of whales. Baleen whales, orcas, dolphins and porpoises are all cetaceans. Just to keep the world interesting, so are narwhals.

Emil Palm's reimagined poster for Orson Welles's *Moby Dick*.

6

Moby Dick

"The Killer is never hunted. I never heard what sort of oil he has. Exception might be taken to the name bestowed upon this whale, on the ground of its indistinctness. For we are all killers, on land and on sea; Bonapartes and Sharks included."

—Herman Melville, *Moby Dick; or, The Whale*

Whales of all types were especially infamous in the nineteenth century, when streetlamps were lit with whale oil. The most notorious weren't killers but sperm whales.

In 1820 an 85-foot (26-meter), 16,000-pound (7,257-kilogram) sperm whale stalked, attacked and sank the American whaling ship *Essex*. The survivors shared the story of the whale who demolished their 265-ton (240-tonne) floating factory by ramming it head on—twice. Twenty crewmen escaped on three small whaling boats. Captain George Pollard Jr. claimed his men almost died again when a "killer whale" rammed their boat and took a bite out of it. This is a story I find as hard to swallow as an orca would a lifeboat.

After ninety-two days at sea only eight men survived, several by resorting to cannibalism. One survivor was the captain, who admitted he ate his nephew. Pollard lost a second ship a few years later. After this he was declared a "Jonah" after one of the Old Testament's least lucky characters—a man who was swallowed by a very big fish (often called a whale).

The whale who sank the *Essex* was infamous. But the world's most famous and feared whale was an albino sperm whale who whalers named Mocha Dick. The legendary killer sperm whale received part of his name after shaking loose a harpoon off the coast of Mocha Island near Chile. And Dick? Whalers gave the scariest whales the names of ordinary men to make them seem less frightening. But this Dick haunted whalers thanks to tales he had killed thirty men.

American author (and whaler) Herman Melville heard the stories of Pollard's shipwreck and Mocha's might and put the two together.

In Melville's book the *Essex* became the *Pequod*. The captain was Ahab. Mocha turned into Moby. *Moby Dick; or, The Whale* was released in 1851 and received such bad reviews you'd think a sperm whale wrote it. During Melville's lifetime, *Moby Dick* was his least popular novel. Now it's known as one of the best books of all time.

More than thirty years after Melville's death, Moby Dick became one of the world's most famous monsters. How?

In 1912 Captain Robert Scott reminded people that whales were scary when he led a mission to the Antarctic. His men found themselves on ice floes surrounded by orcas.

A blue whale chasing krill in Monterey Bay, California. JOSH McINNES

Moby Dick snacking on sailors.
A. BURNHAM SHUTE ILLUSTRATION FROM *MOBY DICK; OR, THE WHALE*, C.H. SIMONDS COMPANY, 1892.

The men were with sled dogs. Dog barks sound a lot like seal barks, so maybe that's why the orcas cracked through the ice to attack.

Scott wrote: "One after another their huge hideous heads shot vertically into the air through the cracks which they had made. As they reared them to a height of 6 or 8 feet (1.8 or 2.4 meters) it was possible to see their tawny head markings, their small glistening eyes, and their terrible array of teeth—by far the largest and most terrifying in the world."

But once they saw that there were no seals on the ice, just humans and dogs, the whales swam off.

That didn't stop newspapers from running headlines like "The terror of the Antarctic—a man-killing whale."

The more likely reason *Moby Dick* became a hit, though, was the same reason books often make it big today. The movies.

Scott's team filmed the orcas hunting, and the world saw the killers on-screen—acting like killers.

In 1926 American movie star John Barrymore played a heroic Ahab in a silent movie called *The Sea Beast*. Barrymore wasn't just an actor. If *People* magazine had existed in 1926, he would have been called "The Sexiest Man Alive." *The Sea Beast* made such a splash that Barrymore remade the same movie (with sound) four years later as *Moby Dick*.

At the same time Barrymore battled Moby on-screen, American author Zane Grey wrote about the terror of seeing an orca up close. He called orcas "the most ferocious and terrible of all the wolves of the sea. They are equally dangerous to man."

Barrymore's Moby swam right into the Disney version of *Pinocchio*. The puppet who wanted to be a real live boy found himself in the belly of the beast after escaping Pleasure Island. In the original fairy tale the monster was a shark, but thanks to Moby Dick, whales were the stuff of nightmares.

For over a century, when most people in North America and Europe imagined whales, they pictured Moby Dick—an unstoppable force of nature. A monster. Then the world met Moby Doll.

A sperm whale's tail shows the size of Moby Dick from the classic whale tale.
KJERSTI JOERGENSEN/SHUTTERSTOCK.COM

Moby Doll arrives in Vancouver on the
end of a harpoon line.
COURTESY OF TERRY McLEOD

Moby Doll

"Despite our much-valued ability to probe the secrets of the universe, we have so far failed to probe the mystery of the mind of the whale."

—Farley Mowat, *A Whale for the Killing*

Chimo and Haida making a splash at Sealand in Victoria, BC, in 1972.
JOHN COLBY

The Age of Aquariums

"To endow animals with human emotions has long been a scientific taboo. But if we do not, we risk missing something fundamental, about both animals and us."

—Frans de Waal, primatologist and ethologist

Cuddles

The first captive orca in Europe was named Cuddles, but he wasn't cuddly. After being caught in the Salish Sea in 1968 he was flown to England. Cuddles was displayed at the Dudley Zoo in the West Midlands, then moved to a small tank in an aquarium in Yorkshire. Cuddles attacked and injured two trainers. He became so dangerous that cleaners would only enter his tank in a shark cage. He died in 1974 due to heart problems and an infection.

The world's next captive orca became a movie star.

Less than a year after Moby Doll drowned, two salmon fishermen checked their net after a storm and discovered they'd accidentally caught a pair of orcas.

Before Moby Doll, the men might have shot both whales to stop them from eating salmon. But they'd heard that crazy aquarium owners were willing to pay $20,000 for a live killer whale. With dreams of a quick, easy payday, the fishermen put out word they had two whales.

Despite all the interest in Moby Doll, no one was ready to pay $20,000 for an orca. The older orca found a way out of the net but wouldn't leave the younger one behind. The older orca kept trying to show the little orca the way out. When the young whale finally swam away, the older orca was trapped. After the younger orca escaped, the fishermen set a deadline. Unless someone came up with $8,000 right away, they were cutting their killer whale loose.

Ted Griffin, who ran an aquarium on Seattle's waterfront, had loved orcas since his childhood. He'd dreamed of one day riding a killer whale. Griffin collected $8,000 from his neighbors who ran the other businesses on the piers. He promised they'd all get rich from the tourists after he brought home his star. Griffin named his new 23-foot (7-meter) male whale Namu after the town in British Columbia where the whale was caught.

When his star arrived at Seattle Harbor, people filled the pier. Small boats and private planes surrounded his floating pen. A band played. Dancers danced. Seattle went wild for Namu. Griffin was soon not only hand feeding Namu, but swimming with him. A screenwriter started scripting the story of a misunderstood orca. In the movie, the orca was caught by a scientist in a small fishing village where fishermen wanted to kill the monster.

There was a Namu song and a Namu dance.

Namu became a star at the Seattle Marine Aquarium, and Griffin partnered with Don Goldsberry, another aquarium operator, to capture a friend—and possibly a mate—for Namu.

After a failed attempt to catch an orca with a harpoon (the whale was badly injured), they caught a pair with a net. Once the orcas were trapped, the men realized they'd captured the whale they'd harpooned and her daughter. The mother died. Griffin added weights to the dead orca so no one would know he'd killed a mother in front of her calf. When he was asked where the mom went, Griffin told reporters she was scared off by tourists.

Orcas being lassoed at Penn Cove in 1971. WASHINGTON STATE ARCHIVES

One of the earliest Shamus on display
at SeaWorld.
JOHN COLBY

Once the baby was in the aquarium, the newly orphaned 14-foot (4.25-meter) orca attacked Namu and Griffin. Griffin had no way of knowing this, but the baby orca and Namu were from two different worlds. Namu was a *northern resident*, and the baby was a southern resident. These two whales never would have been this close together in the ocean. Rather than risk injury to his star—or himself—Griffin sold his new baby to SeaWorld in San Diego.

SeaWorld wanted to buy the name Namu, but Griffin wouldn't sell it. So SeaWorld named her Shamu—*She* plus *Namu*.

Namu soon died from an infection caused by the polluted water around Seattle's harbor. He'd survived just over a year in captivity. When Namu's body was examined, a bullet was found in his blubber. Like so many orcas in the Salish Sea, Namu had been shot.

Griffin and Goldsberry wanted a new whale for their aquarium. The men also realized there might be big bucks in catching orcas for other aquariums.

Until 1976, every captive orca in the world had been caught in the Salish Sea. At least 270 orcas were captured (many more than once). At least 12 died as a result of orca hunts. Fifty orcas (almost all southern residents) were displayed in tanks around the world.

One orca who collected frequent capture miles was Ocean Sun. In the summer of 1970 she and her family were gathering for a superpod off the coast of Whidbey Island in Washington State when a bomb went off. As the whales scattered in panic there was another explosion, then another. As each bomb rocked the water, the sound deafened and disoriented the orcas. The whales raced toward the harbor to escape.

ORCA BITES

Calypso

The first orca displayed in France arrived in 1970. The six-year-old northern resident was captured in the Salish Sea and flown to England. Then she was flown to Marineland of Antibes. She died there later that year of a lung infection.

Ocean Sun was swimming beside her daughter. Back then she wasn't the oldest orca, so the matriarch may have been J pod's leader, Granny. Granny would have been with her son, Ruffles. Male orcas rarely leave their moms alone.

All the other orcas would have watched the matriarch. Wherever she went, the others would follow.

Of course, Granny didn't know the explosives were designed to frighten her family, not kill them.

When the explosions stopped, the orcas squeaked and squealed. They used echolocation to figure out where they were and what was going on. The more whales there are, the more pings they send out and the more they can "see." Because this sense is shared, all the orcas may have realized the horrible truth at the same time. They were trapped.

The boats chasing them into Penn Cove had nets. The men on the boats had metal lassos to grab the orcas they wanted.

Griffin and Goldsberry's crew caught Ocean Sun and pretty much every other southern resident. But people nearby saw the whales panic, heard their screams, sensed their pain.

Two men, who wanted to help the whales, slit the nets with a bread knife, but nets are almost impossible for whales to see or echolocate. This may explain why orcas won't try to escape from nets by jumping over them.

The would-be heroes didn't know that. So they never would have imagined that their rescue attempt would lead to three young whales getting tangled in the ropes and drowning. Once again, Griffin and his crew sank the bodies with weights.

Even though people didn't know about the dead whales, the sight and sounds of families fighting for freedom were horrifying.

Orcas captured at Penn Cove in Washington State. WASHINGTON STATE ARCHIVES

Aquariums didn't want older whales like Granny or Ocean Sun. They wanted babies who could be trained. Seven of the youngest whales—three females and four males—were sold, including one of Ocean Sun's daughters. She was flown to a tank on the other side of the continent. The Miami Seaquarium named her Lolita. She's now old enough to be a grandmother and lives in a pool in Florida not much bigger than some of the boats full of people taking photos of her mother.

Griffin set the other orcas free. But the tide had turned against his business, and it became a tidal wave two months later when the bodies of the sunken baby whales floated to the surface.

Ruffles (J1), who had ridges on his dorsal fin, swimming in the Salish Sea. VAL SHORE

Terry McLeod meeting a newly captured orca. ANNE CLEMENCE

9

Thinking Bigg

"I believe the future of killer whale research will likely continue in much the same way for some time to come. That is, individual initiative and imagination to recognize the research opportunity and then the commitment to check it out."

—Michael Bigg

Tumbo's dorsal fin is curved because of scoliosis. MICHELLE RACHEL

In 350 BCE the Greek philosopher Aristotle wrote that it was possible to tell dolphins apart by the nicks in their tails. In the 1970s, when Canadian scientist Michael Bigg suggested this could work with orcas, the idea seemed unbelievable. Yes, African researchers were identifying apes and monkeys on sight, but orcas?

Bigg was studying seals and sea lions when he was asked to feed a seal to Moby Doll. Moby wasn't interested in seals, but Bigg was interested in Moby. He began to study the whale's breathing. After Moby died, Bigg examined the body and helped reassemble the skeleton.

As orca hunting heated up on both sides of the Canada–US border, the Canadian government wanted to know how many orcas were out there. Fishermen were sure there were thousands, maybe tens of thousands, because they saw so many dorsals. What fishermen didn't realize was that they were seeing the same dorsals over and over and over.

Bigg discovered and proved that the shape of and markings on both the dorsal fins and the saddle patch are unique. He also proved that orca skin doesn't recover from nicks and cuts. A scratch or bite an orca receives at birth never goes away. In the early days of his research, Bigg cut two notches in a wild orca's dorsal to prove his theory. That orca became known as K1 or Taku.

To keep track of the whales he saw, Bigg took pictures of their left sides. This was because the steering wheel of his boat, *The Brown Bomber*, was on the right side, so it was easier to take photos of the left sides of the whales. Bigg assigned each new pod he met a letter, starting with A (the whales in A pod became known as northern residents).

Each orca also got a number, based on the order in which they swam into his line of sight. Soon Bigg and his team started giving nicknames to whales they could easily spot. Sharky (A25) had a dorsal that looked like a shark fin. Nicola (A2) had a nicked fin. Stubbs (A1) had a partial dorsal. In 1971 Bigg ran the first ever orca survey. His team sent 15,000 forms to people willing to watch the waters off the coasts of Alaska, British Columbia, Washington State, Oregon and California. His plan was to count how many killer whales were spotted on July 26, 1971. The numbers were shocking. Instead of tens of thousands of orcas, the official count was 549. The next year he did a similar survey, with almost identical results.

Mike Bigg examining an orca in Pedder Bay in 1973. JOHN COLBY

If Bigg was right, orca captures had to stop.

The government in Washington State wasn't sold on Bigg's count or his science. They hired Ken Balcomb to figure out how many orcas there were on the American side of the border. In 1976 Balcomb confirmed that the numbers were that low and agreed that it was possible to identify every orca in the Salish Sea on sight.

Like many people who study orcas, Balcomb fell in love with them. He moved to Friday Harbor (on San Juan Island in the United States) and helped open a whale museum. His goal was to raise awareness about the orcas. He's run an orca population survey every year since his first one.

To help raise money for his museum, Balcomb and his friends started giving the orcas catchier nicknames, like Granny. The nicknames stuck. Soon the public was invited to help, and names became cuter. Recent southern resident names include Kiki, Nova, Racer, Yoda and Cappuccino.

As Bigg followed the orcas, he realized that not only did pods stick together, but certain pods stuck to specific sections of the Salish Sea. Then, because he and his team knew who was who, they realized there were two types of orcas—mammal eaters and fish eaters. He named the fish eaters "residents," since they didn't travel much.

He called the mammal eaters "transients" because they hunted for food over a much wider area. These two types of orcas didn't just eat different foods: they hunted—and lived—in different ways. Residents travel as large family units, and they're curvier than mammal eaters, chatty and playful. They look and act like really big dolphins.

Transients split into smaller groups and hunt like the infamous wolves of the sea. Transient orcas are sleeker than residents, their dorsals sharper, their behavior more like the killer whales who inspired horror stories.

Scientists eventually realized just how different these whales are when genetic tests proved these two types of orcas had not bred with each other for over 700,000 years.

One of Bigg's fellow researchers, John Ford, suggested that pods might have not only different habits, but also different ways of communicating. It was Bigg's turn to doubt an idea. Fortunately for whale lovers everywhere, Ford kept listening.

Scarlet practicing her breaches in the Salish Sea. CLINT RIVERS

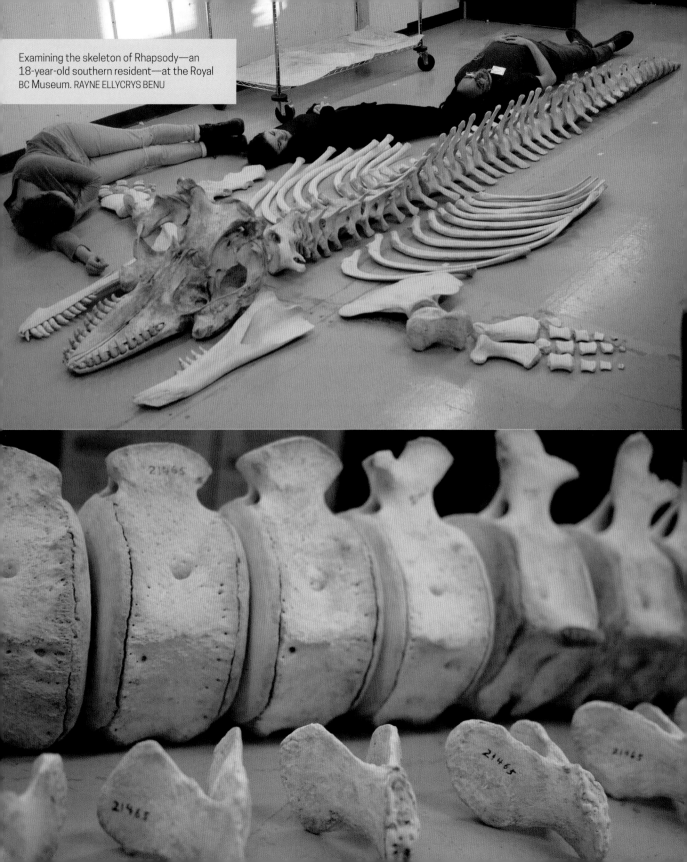

Examining the skeleton of Rhapsody—an 18-year-old southern resident—at the Royal BC Museum. RAYNE ELLYCRYS BENU

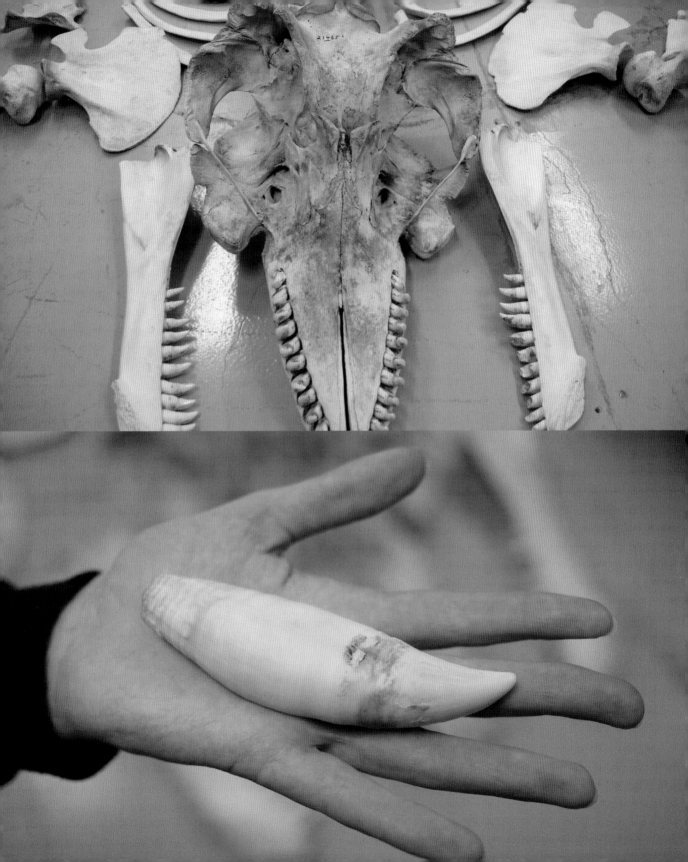

Bill Reid's iconic orca sculpture *Skaana* outside the Vancouver Aquarium.
RAYNE ELLYCRYS BENU

10

Listening to Orcas

"Killer whales are the most amazing animals that currently live on this planet."

—Robert Pitman, American marine ecologist

The first time John Ford saw a whale, he was terrified. He was enjoying a perfect day on the family speedboat with his parents when a pod of orcas surfaced. The whales were approaching their 15-foot (4.5-meter) boat, and his parents thought they were doomed. "We were all terrified, including my father. These were wolves of the sea; they would eat anything, including people, without hesitation. If they bumped the boat, and we tipped over, we'd be consumed right away." Everyone on the boat held on to the sides and hoped for the best.

The orcas swam toward the boat, then under it, then kept swimming. The Fords believed they had survived a near-death experience and not what most people today would consider the best whale-watching day *ever*.

When John was nine, the Vancouver Aquarium captured Moby Doll. His dad took John to meet the legendary monster, who didn't look very monstrous. "It was a big dry dock and a very small whale, sort of looking rather lonely in there."

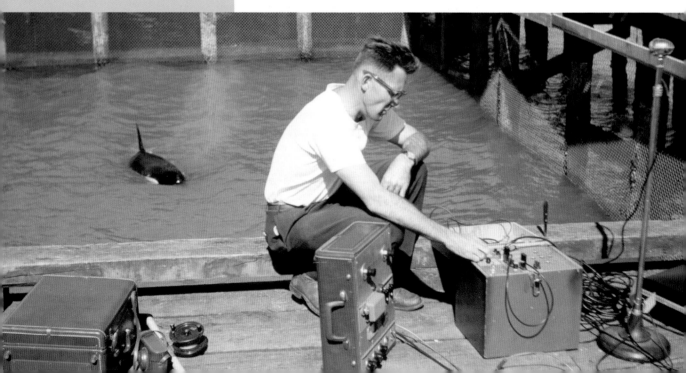

Vince Penfold from the Vancouver Aquarium listening to Moby Doll and trying to compile an orca dictionary.
COURTESY OF TERRY McLEOD

Ford's mom was a volunteer guide at the aquarium, and John followed in her footsteps. After his first year of university, Ford took a summer job there, sweeping up the litter people left after watching whale shows. Murray Newman, the director of the aquarium, was famous for sneaking up on everyone who worked there and asking, "So what have we learned today?" Ford decided to learn something and began listening to Skana and Hyak. The next year he started working as a trainer, and he kept listening.

His focus in university was studying orca sounds. He borrowed the old equipment the Canadian navy had used to record Moby Doll and listened to old tapes of Moby Doll to study his calls (also known as *vocalizations*). "They really are unusual sounds and a little bit sad."

He kept studying vocalizations and eventually went out to meet whales in the wild with scientists like Bigg.

Just as Bigg identified different behaviors, Ford discovered different sounds. Some whales, like humpbacks and bowheads, have long, complicated vocalizations that sound like songs. Orcas sound less like they're singing than speaking. And Ford didn't think A pod sounded like B or C pod. The idea of another species having any type of language was, and still is, controversial. But the idea that families could have their own styles of speech seemed impossible.

"Mike Bigg used to laugh and say I had no business even speculating that these things had different dialects at the family level. It was just through my ignorance that I proposed that." Ford had a theory, but most of the recordings in the world were the ones he was making. There was nothing to compare the sounds to until the day in 1978 when he placed his hydrophone by the side of the boat and heard J pod for the first time.

ORCA BITES

Blowholes

A blowhole on an orca works like a nose on a human. Orcas breathe oxygen like we do and need to surface for air just like we do when we're swimming. The blowhole allows orcas to breathe while they are still partly underwater.

He'd found Moby Doll's family.

He had proof of dialects and had discovered something amazing about orca culture: the dialects are passed on from generation to generation.

This also helped prove that orcas are one of the only mammals able to learn and reproduce sounds. Orcas are now known to copy the sounds of dolphins and sea lions, likely to trick them when they're hunting.

In 2018 researchers in France proved orcas can also copy humans. After teaching Wilkie, a 14-year-old captive orca, the meaning of *copy*, her trainers taught the orca to copy ten words. She learned *hello, bye bye* and the name of her trainer. Once Wilkie understood what the trainers

J50 near Lime Kiln Point, San Juan Island, WA, with other females in her family on August 11, 2018.
KATY FOSTER/NATIONAL OCEANIC AND ATMOSPHERIC ADMINISTRATION/ DEPARTMENT OF COMMERCE

wanted, it took her a maximum of seventeen tries to learn a word. She nailed *hello* and *one, two, three* on her first try. Considering how quickly she picked up the words, it might be interesting to know how quickly she could learn their meanings. But that wasn't part of the study.

That level of learning wouldn't be surprising since dolphins have learned to understand up to 100 words of English. To date, humans still don't know one word of orca-ish.

LISTENING TO US

When Sam Burich wanted to make friends with Moby Doll, he played his harmonica to share music. Paul Spong also

Ken Balcomb, founder of the Center for Whale Research, waves at the camera and the whales. CLINT RIVERS

experimented with music when he was working with Skana and Hyak. Spong wanted to know if the whales would like music as a reward instead of food. They did.

He played all types of music, and the orcas seemed to enjoy everything—including the Rolling Stones. One surprise was that they responded best when they heard new songs. Spong believed the whales had such a good acoustic memory that they always wanted the next tune.

He also experimented with playing music for wild whales. The best response he got was when a pod followed his boat as a Vancouver rock band played for them.

In 1970 an orca made an album. Haida was a captive in Sealand of the Pacific in Victoria, BC. He shared a small tank with an albino orca named Chimo. After Chimo's death Haida stopped eating and barely moved. Sealand tried everything to get Haida to eat—including getting him drunk on Guinness beer. When nothing worked Paul Spong suggested they try music.

Jazz musician Paul Horn was invited to play his flute for the grieving whale. Horn played sad songs for a week, and Haida didn't respond. Finally Horn spoke to the whale and told him he'd only come back one more time. The next day when he played, Haida started swimming again. Horn put down his flute and fed Haida a herring. It was the first food Haida had eaten in a month.

For the next five days Haida followed Horn as he walked around the pool, playing his flute. He recorded several songs to which he added the orca's calls. When the album was released he called it *Haida and Paul Horn*. He also released a video of their encounters called *Haida and Paul Horn: The Adventures of a Killer Whale and a Jazz Musician*.

ORCA BITES

Listen to the whales

You can listen to orca vocalizations on lots of websites. Try the Right Whale Listening Network or even YouTube.

Paul Spong playing music for Hyak in Victoria, BC.
REX WEYLER/GREENPEACE

Orca Procession, painting by Robert Bateman.

11

What's in a Name?

"Every meat-eating creature is a killer. Orca is much more dignified. Dignity is the name that applies to these creatures. They are big and very impressive in their speed, intelligence and power."

—Robert Bateman, Canadian artist and naturalist

ORCA BITES

Orca on the rocks

The world's biggest orcas aren't in the water but on the rocks. There's an image of an orca carved into the rocks in southern Peru that's over 200 feet (61 meters) long. The *geoglyph*—an image made of carefully arranged stones—was likely created by the Paracas and Nazca peoples, who considered orcas gods. They were creating orca images back in 800 BCE. In northern Norway there's an orca *petroglyph*—an image carved into stone. The Norwegian orca is believed to be between 6,000 and 9,000 years old. In Wrangell, Alaska, there's an 8,000-year-old orca likely carved by the Tlingit people. Because of the 40 orca images in the area, the area is known as Petroglyph Beach State Historic Park.

The scientific name for killer whale is *Orcinus orca* (demon from hell). So the only reason *orca* sounds friendlier than *killer* is that most people today don't know Latin.

Basque fishermen used the term *ballena assesina*, which means "whale assassin." Some people suspect this is the secret origin of the name killer whale. Argentina uses the same name, with the same meaning and a different spelling: *ballena asesina*.

Germans call orcas *Mörderwal*. *Wal* means "whale," and *Mörder* means "assassin, killer or murderer."

The Tsartlip people in British Columbia call orcas KEL□OLEMEĆEN, which means "killer whales."

Aleuts of Kodiak Island call orcas *polossatik*—"the feared one."

When I was at the whaling museum in Sarpsborg, Norway, the tour guide said one orca name means "signpost." The reason: the whales who hung around Norway were herring eaters—like almost every Norwegian human I've ever met. When Norwegian fishermen saw orcas' dorsals, they followed them as if they were signposts announcing, "This way to herring."

That's when I realized that one reason the names for orcas change from place to place is that different human cultures know different orca cultures.

Some people saw only fish-eating orcas, who seem friendly and adorable (unless you're the fish they eat). Other people witnessed mammal-eating orcas ripping humpback whales and sea lions to shreds.

The people of Byzantium (an ancient Greek colony in what is now Istanbul) called orcas *krios thalattios*: sea-rams. They named one orca who "annoyed" them for over fifty years Porphyrius (purple). This was a royal color, indicating that people may have considered the orca ocean royalty.

The indigenous Ainu in Japan use the name *Repun Kamuy*, which means "God of offshore." Another Japanese name, *Repun Kamui*, means "master of the open seas."

Favorite nicknames in North America include blackfish, swordfish or grampus. Yes, I think grampus sounds silly too. It may come from English people hearing the French words *grand poisson*, which mean "big fish." It may also come from the Latin *craspicis*, which means "fat fish." The British use the same names—except for blackfish, which is just North American slang.

In Quebec orca names include *épaulard* and *espadon*—"orca gladiator" and "swordfish."

The world's biggest orca—a geoglyph in Peru. JOHNY ISLA

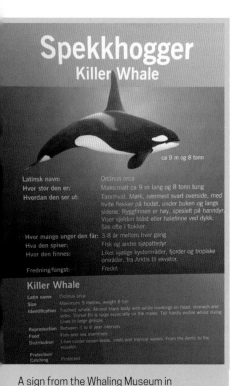

Spekkhogger
Killer Whale

ca 9 m og 8 tonn

Latinsk navn: Orcinus orca
Hvor stor den er: Maksimalt ca 9 m lang og 8 tonn tung
Hvordan den ser ut: Tannhval. Mørk, nærmest svart overside, med hvite flekker på hodet, under buken og langs sidene. Ryggfinnen er høy, spesielt på hanndyr. Viser sjelden blåst eller halefinne ved dykk. Ses ofte i flokker.

Hvor mange unger den får: 3-8 år mellom hver gang
Hva den spiser: Fisk og andre sjøpattedyr
Hvor den finnes: Liker kjølige kystområder, fjorder og tropiske områder, fra Arktis til ekvator.

Fredning/fangst: Fredet

Killer Whale
Latin name: Orcinus orca
Size: Maximum 9 metres, weight 8 ton
Identification: Toothed whale. Almost black body with white markings on head, stomach and sides. Dorsal fin is large especially on the males. Tail hardly visible whilst diving. Lives in large groups.
Reproduction: Between 3 to 8 year intervals
Food: Fish and sea mammals
Distribution: Likes cooler ocean areas, inlets and tropical waters. From the Arctic to the equator.
Protection/ Catching: Protected

A sign from the Whaling Museum in Sandefjord, Norway. MARK LEIREN-YOUNG

France uses *épaulard* and *orque* but adds *épée de mer* (sword of the sea).

German names for orcas include s*chwertwal* (sword-whale) and *schwertfisch* (swordfish).

Icelandic names include *háhyrningur* (high horn) and *sverdfiscur* (swordfish). The orcas in Iceland were considered *illhveli*—"evil whales." *Sverðhvalur*—possibly orcas—were known enemies of blue whales. Whales may have been dubbed evil because they were scary or because they weren't tasty. Sirún Almeida at Whales of Iceland Marine Research Institute says, "Remember that Icelanders believe in trolls and elves, so everything for them is magic and monstrous, including sea creatures."

In the Netherlands orcas are also called *zvaardwalvis* (sword-whale) and *zvaardvis* (swordfish).

Denmark's orca names include *hvalhund* (whale-dog) and *sværdval* (sword-whale). They also use *spækhugger* (blubber-chopper). So do the Swedes and Norwegians.

The Russian name *kosatka* means "scythe," which is a tool with a large curved blade.

So what's with all the sword references?

It's all about the shape of the dorsal, which some people think looks kind of swordlike.

The number-one name in Madagascar is *tsingy*, which means "summit" or "mountain" and also refers to the shape of the dorsal.

The Yupik people near the Bering Strait called orcas *Kăk-whăn'-û-ghăt Kĭg-û-lu'-nĭk* and said that when the whales wanted to hunt on land they would shape-shift into wolves.

The Inuit also talk about the *Akhlut*, an orca spirit who became a wolf—or part wolf—on land. The Chuckhi in Russia also say orcas transform into wolves.

Settlers in these areas may not have believed that orcas could shape-shift, but a common nickname among them was "wolves of the sea."

The Kwakwakw'wakw Nation's word for orcas is *maxinuxw*, which means "side-by-side tribe" and refers to the way these whales sometimes swim.

Australians cut to the chase these days and just call them killers—although Australia's Koori people, the Yuin, refer to them as *beowas*, which means "brothers" or "kin."

In the Xwlemi Chosen language of the Lummi Nation, which lives near the coast of the Salish Sea, orcas are called *qw'e lh'ol' me chen*—"our relations who live under the water."

NAMES HAVE POWER

What we call orcas—and other animals—helps determine how we treat them. It's easier to get humans to care about orcas than about killers.

If you live with a cat or a dog or a giraffe, I'll bet you don't call it "cat," "dog" or "giraffe." You've probably given it a name, like Kiki, Oreo or Princess Angeline (which are all names of J pod orcas). And once animals have names, it's easier to see them the way we see people—as individuals.

In most types of law, personhood is a key concept.

The US Constitution originally declared that only adult white men who owned land were persons. Women and non-white men had limited or no legal rights. Like orcas, they were property, like your shoes or your bike. Most countries had similar laws to restrict certain humans from having legal rights.

In some places, like New Zealand and India, certain rivers have been declared persons. This means humans have to respect and protect these rivers. In 2018 a

Rayne Ellycrys Benu visiting Granny's Way in Friday Harbor, WA. MARK LEIREN-YOUNG

thirteen-year-old Canadian, Autumn Peltier, told the United Nations General Assembly to give water the same rights as people: "We need to acknowledge our waters with personhood so we can protect our waters."

Legally, orcas are objects. Things.

Legally, all animals are things.

Right now orcas—and other animals—have roughly the same rights as this book. If you ripped the book in half, I'd be upset, but as long as you paid for it, no one would arrest you.

To have legal rights, an orca has to be declared a person. If they were persons, we could no longer treat them like they don't matter.

Animal rights lawyers in the United States are fighting to declare some apes persons. There are other court cases around the world arguing that cetaceans should have the right to move freely. Some scientists even signed a cetacean bill of rights (see page 150). You can sign it too at the Cetacean Rights website.

WHALES ARE PEOPLE (OR PERSONS) TOO

There are two words that come up all the time when discussing our relationship with animals. And you need to know these words to understand an all-new word that I love.

Anthrop is Latin for "human." Adding an *o* on the end of the word creates *anthropo*, which means "humanlike." *Anthropology* is the study of human societies.

Anthropocentrism is the belief that humans are the rock stars of all living things. This is not exactly the dictionary definition, but basically it's the belief that *we rule*!

The book of Genesis says God gave man dominion over all other living things. How you interpret this depends on

Activist Autumn Peltier fighting for the planet. LINDA ROY

how you define *dominion*. Some people translate it as "responsibility for." Most people believe it means "ownership of," which is where some people get the idea that animals exist just for us to use.

Anthropomorphizing means thinking a god, animal or thing has emotions or experiences similar to ours. So suggesting a whale can sing, an ape can laugh or a dog can be sad is anthropomorphizing. This is considered extremely unscientific. When a scientist says someone is anthropomorphizing, they are almost always dissing them.

Giving an animal a human name is often considered anthropomorphizing or humanizing. It is also a key to getting humans to care about animals, since people are more likely to fall in love with Ocean Sun or Granny than L25 or J2.

One of the first things humans do when we want to devalue someone is take away their names. That's why people in jail have their names replaced by numbers.

I anthropomorphize. A lot.

I think orcas dance, humpbacks sing and animals of all types feel emotions—or something similar enough that we shouldn't have to make up new words so we can pretend their experiences are alien. I think anyone who doesn't believe animals have feelings, emotions or intelligence is suffering from *anthropodenial*.

Anthropodenial means that anyone who doesn't get that animals have feelings, emotions or intelligence isn't paying attention. This word was created in 2001 by Frans de Waal, a scientist studying monkeys. He defined it as "a blindness to the human-like characteristics of other animals, or the animal-like characteristics of ourselves."

This is a form of reality blindness that does not seem to affect any Indigenous cultures anywhere.

ORCA BITES

Masters of the sea

The Nivkh people in Russia considered orcas masters of the sea and saw them as protectors and helpers of the sea gods because orcas killed larger whales. Not only would the Nivkh not kill orcas, but if one washed up onshore, they would honor the body and bury it in a special wooden house.

Some people think orcas are big dolphins, but dolphins are small whales. CLINT RIVERS

IS AN ORCA REALLY A WHALE?

If you walk around with this book long enough, someone will tell you, "Orcas are not really whales—they are the largest member of the dolphin family."

This is true.

Sort of.

It's also false.

Isn't science awesome?

Pretty much every dictionary definition of *whale* describes a "very large marine mammal with a tail fin and a blowhole." That sure sounds like an orca to me.

When Herman Melville listed every species of whale in *Moby Dick*, he included "the Killer."

There are more than seventy kinds of whales who have teeth. The largest are sperm whales (like Moby Dick). Orcas are among the largest.

So why does anyone think they're dolphins?

In 1735 Swedish *botanist* Carl Linnaeus published the first volume of his book *Systema Naturae*. This pretty much created the rules scientists still use for categorizing living things. These rules are known as *taxonomy*.

He originally called orcas *Delphinus orca* (demon dolphin) and classified them as belonging to the family Delphinidae. As you can guess from the name, this category includes dolphins. When he found out more about killer whales, he changed their name to *Orcinus orcus* (demon from hell) but didn't bother to change their category.

Here's the thing. Carl didn't spend much, if any, time around whales.

In the first nine volumes of his book, he said whales were fish.

He didn't realize whales were mammals until his book's tenth edition. That was when all whales, dolphins and

Orcas traveling in Alaskan waters.
THOMAS JEFFERSON/NATIONAL OCEANIC AND ATMOSPHERIC ADMINISTRATION/DEPARTMENT OF COMMERCE

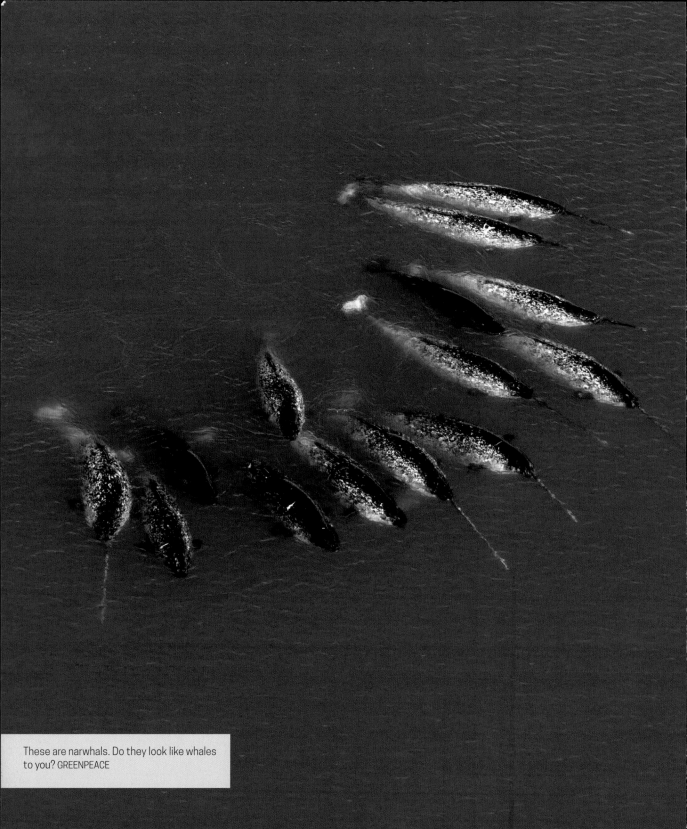

These are narwhals. Do they look like whales to you? GREENPEACE

porpoises were classified as cetaceans, which comes from the Latin word *cetus*. *Cetus* means—you guessed it—"whale."

Some people will tell you killer whales and short-finned pilot whales are really big dolphins—because they are Delphinidae—but it's more accurate to say dolphins and porpoises are really small whales, because that's what cetacean means.

Meanwhile, Linnaeus lists narwhals—yes, narwhals—as *toothed whales*. Have you ever seen a narwhal? Check out the picture on the facing page. Does that look like a whale to you?

And just as orcas and pilots are Delphinidae, the most whale-like whales on the planet (blue whales) are *rorquals*. This was a term used to classify big baleens.

So if someone tells you orcas are dolphins, tell them that following their logic, blue whales aren't whales either. Or blow their minds by explaining that dolphins are whales.

This is a blue whale. But is it really a whale or a rorqual? LISA CONGER AND MARJORIE FOSTER/ NATIONAL OCEANIC AND ATMOSPHERIC ADMINISTRATION/DEPARTMENT OF COMMERCE

An orca hunting herring in Norway.
ALESSANDRO DE MADDALENA

12

Orca Intelligence

"To have a huge, friendly whale willingly approach your boat and look you straight in the eye is without doubt one of the most extraordinary experiences on the planet."

—Mark Carwardine, co-author, *Last Chance to See*

The ancient Greeks thought the earth was the center of the universe. About 2,300 years ago, Ptolemy (an astronomer, among many other things) came up with a model showing how all the planets and stars revolved around our world. Of course, everyone also "knew" the world was flat. And doubting these "truths" was punishable by death.

Most humans didn't just agree that we were the top of the *food chain*; we were the only animals who were intelligent, had emotions, could use tools and were self-aware and compassionate. The theory (which some people still believe) was that humans had intelligence and emotions, but animals just had instincts.

Not all people have been on board with this worldview. Many Indigenous cultures saw animals as family, if not gods. But the people running most of the planet thought nature was something to be tamed and that animals just existed for our benefit.

MIRROR, MIRROR

Tests of animal intelligence were designed to see if animals could copy us. So even though an ape was unlikely to find a candy machine in the forest, we'd test apes to see if they could use machines. Apes and other animals had to prove how smart they were by figuring out human technology, tools and rules. Then researchers would compare them to human children. There weren't any tests in which children were sent to the jungle to see how well they could survive as apes.

One test designed to prove humans are the best and brightest on the planet is *mirror self-recognition*. The theory is that if an animal can recognize itself in the mirror—

Frejya versus the mirror.
RAYNE ELLYCRYS BENU

like we do—then it is "self-aware." The subject would get a mark put on its face, and the scientist would see if the animal cleaned up the smudge. Humans start to recognize their reflections when they're about eighteen months old. Or maybe that's when babies start to care about smudges?

Since mirrors aren't a big thing in nature, it strikes me as an odd test to determine what, how or if nonhumans are thinking. I don't know if my cat, Frejya, recognizes herself in the mirror, but I do know she stopped attacking the kitty in the mirror not long after realizing it wasn't fighting back. If she still thought it was another cat, she'd have trashed

Moby Doll's brain next to a human brain. This image helped launch the first Greenpeace campaign to save the whales. REX WEYLER/GREENPEACE

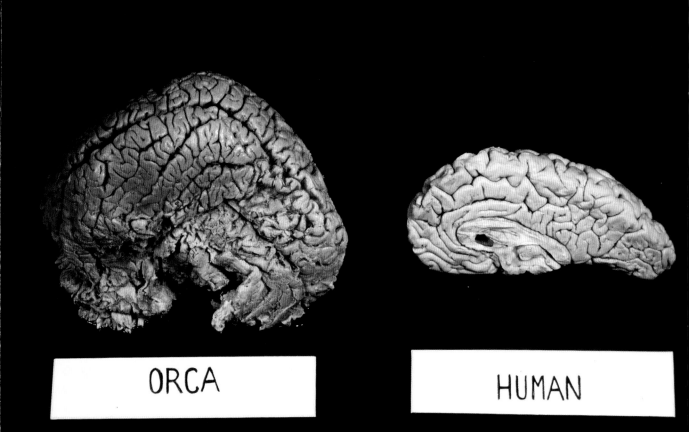

ORCA

HUMAN

Orca brains

Orcas have the second-biggest brain of ocean mammals. Only sperm whales—like Moby Dick—have bigger brains. Orca brains can weigh up to 15 pounds (6.8 kilograms). Orcas learn quickly and also learn things we don't expect them to. An orca at SeaWorld San Diego watched a boy outside his tank spin and then copied the move. Orcas who live near bottlenose dolphins have learned to mimic their calls. And Luna, an orca who liked to hang out with humans, did a perfect impersonation of a boat engine.

every mirror in our house, because that's just how Frejya rolls. But since 1970 the mirror test has been scientific proof of "self-awareness."

When it comes to claiming humans are the only species on earth who can do or feel certain things, cetaceans have always been a challenge. It's easier to imagine that animals who look like us act like us.

Cetaceans couldn't pass the mirror test, which was considered proof they weren't as clever as their fans thought. It clearly had nothing to do with the fact that sight isn't the main way they experience the world. Imagine if orcas were to test our intelligence by seeing how quickly we could find something to eat underwater using echolocation.

In 2001 Diana Reiss of Columbia University and Lori Marino of Emory University found a way to set up a mirror for two bottlenose dolphins—Bayley and Foster. They marked the dolphins with ink. Sure enough, the dolphins became the first animals outside of the ape family to pass the test.

ARE ORCAS LAUGHING AT US?

When the Vancouver Aquarium hired Paul Spong in 1967 to study orca intelligence, his official job was to figure out how well orcas could see. While he was studying two orcas—Skana and Hyak—he quickly became convinced that these whales were testing him. After doing a sight test correctly for days and proving she understood it, Skana gave the wrong answer eighty-two times in a row. These whales weren't just smart but also had a sense of humor.

Skana made sure Spong realized she was in charge after she tested him. Spong would occasionally dangle his feet in the water, and one day Skana grazed them with her teeth.

Spong panicked and pulled his feet out. When he dipped them back in, Skana grazed them again. He pulled his feet out yet again. This continued until Spong stopped pulling out his feet. Skana had trained her trainer.

CAN ORCAS USE TOOLS?

Because our brains are bigger and more complicated than the brains of other animals that early scientists studied, this was considered proof of our superiority. Then scientists saw cetacean brains, and suddenly size didn't matter. Orca brains aren't just bigger than ours but are also more complicated. They have an entire extra lobe for echolocation.

One classic intelligence indicator is tool use. We now know that all sorts of animals use tools—including crows. But how can orcas use tools? They find creative ways to use water.

Orcas in the Arctic trap seals and sea lions on ice floes. The seals and sea lions think they're safe, but the orcas work together to move the ice so their intended meal has nowhere to escape to. Then the orcas work as a team to create waves that wash their victims into the ocean.

Paul Spong at his research institute OrcaLab. REX WEYLER/GREENPEACE

Orcas in Norway work as a team to hunt herring, swimming in ever tighter circles around them to put them in a "tank." Then they slap their tails and knock the small fish out before feasting on them. This hunting move is called carousel feeding.

So orcas transform water into "tools."

The only intelligence tests orcas don't pass are the ones that require hands.

A transient orca at sunset, sending
a valentine though his blowhole.
CLINT RIVERS

13

Orca Love

"It is empathy that not
only makes orcas most
like humans, but perhaps
makes them more
than human."

—David Neiwert, *Of Orcas and Men:
What Killer Whales Can Teach Us*

Humans like to claim we're the only species on earth with emotions. But in 2018 the world watched as southern resident orca Tahlequah (J35) mourned for her calf. Her daughter was the first calf born to the southern residents in three years. The baby swam for less than an hour before dying—likely due to starvation.

Tahlequah balanced the body on her nose for seventeen days, carrying her for more than 1,000 miles (1,609 kilometers). She showed her daughter's body to the other southern residents and the world.

Was it a funeral? Was it a message to us? Whatever her reasons, almost everyone agreed that Tahlequah was grieving for her dead daughter.

Lodie Budwill of the Center for Whale Research watched the other whales join Tahlequah in what looked

J pod lines up for a greeting ceremony with orcas from K pod and L pod. VAL SHORE

like a funeral. "The sun set, the moon rose, and they remained centered in the moonbeam, continuing their circular surfacing. I perceived this to be a ceremony or ritual of some sort. It was no doubt a circle of family love and devotion."

So most people now admit that whales can grieve. Other animals, like elephants, also mourn their dead.

While Tahlequah was carrying her daughter's body, J pod stayed with her. Some people believe the other pod members took turns carrying the body. Others believe that her podmates fed her.

Neither of these actions could be confirmed by official whale watchers, but Tahlequah didn't lose weight even though she wasn't hunting.

One trait humans have always used to prove we are on the top of the evolutionary chain is *altruism*—selfless concern for others. The idea is that only humans are wired to be nice. Scientists and philosophers have claimed this is not just a uniquely human trait but the ultimate proof of our "humanity."

Orcas and some other large whales have *spindle neurons* in their brains. These are cells that process emotions humans thought existed only in apes and us. Spindle neurons have been called the cells that make us human. They're the part of the brain that deals with complex emotions like love, guilt, grief and even embarrassment. Since these are the cells that allow us to feel deeply, isn't it likely they do the same for orcas?

Science relies on what's called *empirical data* (something that can be observed and repeated). Scientists won't use individual incidents (or what they'd call anecdotes) as proof of anything.

Tahlequah carrying her daughter's body.
CENTER FOR WHALE RESEARCH, NMFS PERMIT # 21238

ORCA BITES

Granny

The last known photo of former southern resident matriarch Granny shows her passing a salmon to a young orca. It looks like Granny was starving at the time. No one who knows orcas was surprised Granny did this.

But here are a few anecdotes about orcas behaving in ways that sure seem "human"—like the pair of orcas who risked their lives to stop an unconscious Moby Doll from drowning.

STUMPY

In 1996 an orca with spinal and dorsal injuries was spotted off the coast of Norway. The whale was named Stumpy because, well, people who name orcas seem to lack imagination. Because of his injuries, Stumpy was calf-sized even as an adult. According to the laws of nature, Stumpy should have starved, but adult orcas brought him herring. The most "human"—and shocking—part of Stumpy's story is that at least five different pods brought him food. So this wasn't just family looking after him. Stumpy was fed by strangers who didn't speak his dialect.

Tumbo on the move.
CLINT RIVERS

SIRA

In 2013 in Algoa Bay, South Africa, researchers saw a young orca missing a pectoral and dorsal fin and named him Sira. Instead of leaving the injured orca to die, the pod fed him. In 2017 Sira was spotted again. This time he appeared to be leading his pod on hunts.

TUMBO

In the Salish Sea, a Bigg's whale named Tumbo (T2C2) was born in 1989 with a deformed spine. The older he gets, the more his spine bends out of shape and the tougher it is for him to swim quickly. Like all male orcas, he stays close to his mom. Tsau (T2C) is his pod's matriarch. Since he can't swim fast enough to help hunt, his podmates bring him food. At least one whale usually stays with him when he can't keep up with the pod.

Granny making sure the younger orca gets to eat. This is the last known photo of Granny. NATIONAL OCEANIC AND ATMOSPHERIC ADMINISTRATION/ DEPARTMENT OF COMMERCE

A Bigg's orca hunting a harbor porpoise at full speed. CLINT RIVERS

14

Orca Mysteries

"No wise fish would go anywhere without a porpoise."

—Lewis Carroll, *Alice's Adventures in Wonderland*

ORCA BITES

Dreaming of orcas

In 2016 a Hawaiian fisherman named Clay Ching said that one of his daughters dreamed of orcas. The next day, when he and his daughters were on the water, they spotted a pod just off the coast of Molokai. The three orcas surfaced less than 15 feet (4.5 meters) from their boat. Ching had been fishing and leading tours in those waters for over 50 years. He'd never seen an orca before.

Nature is unpredictable, and the idea that any species would "never" do something may just mean we've never seen it happen.

Everyone knows that orcas never attack one another. Except for that time they did. Southern residents were once spotted getting aggressive with a pod of Bigg's orcas. It's possible the residents were worried about their new baby. But who knows? Scientists have encountered this kind of attack only once, but that doesn't mean it has happened only once.

In 2016 scientists in the Salish Sea saw something that shocked and horrified them—two whales attacking and killing a newborn orca. Again, humans had thought orcas never hurt one another in the wild. Maybe the baby was sick, so the older orcas killed it. Maybe, as scientists on the scene suspected, the young male wanted to breed with the mother. Maybe the two killer whales were just nasty. There's no way for us to find out. But it's a reminder that orcas are still a mystery to us, so never say never.

In 1972, off the coast of Monterey, California, an eighteen-year-old surfer named Hans Kretschmer said he was attacked by an orca who took one bite and swam off. His two friends agreed the attacker was an orca. He needed over 100 stitches. A doctor examined him and agreed that it was an orca bite. But California Fish and Wildlife officers checked the bite marks on the surfboard and wet suit and said it was a shark bite.

Many people have said they felt threatened by orcas, but there is no proof of an orca ever hurting a human in the wild. That doesn't mean it has never happened or that it never will. Some world-renowned orca experts won't get in the ocean with mammal eaters—just in case.

PSYCHIC ORCAS

When the Vancouver Aquarium was waiting to harpoon an orca, Murray Newman mused that whales must be able to sense trouble.

Ted Griffin, the first human to swim with an orca, was certain he'd formed a psychic link with Namu.

If you ask most people who've spent time around orcas whether orcas are psychic, they probably won't like the word because it suggests something supernatural. But almost every researcher has a story about an orca who did something impossible to explain.

When Rayne Ellycrys Benu set out to film Granny for our movie about her, Granny put on a show. As soon as Rayne arrived with her camera, Granny greeted us with a tail-slap, a spy-hop and two *breaches*. We were with two people who'd been watching whales for over twenty years. They'd seen Granny breach only a half dozen times. Ever. But when we arrived, Granny performed like a movie star.

Alexandra Morton wrote in her book *The Company of Whales* that the orcas she was looking to study showed up to greet her on her first day in Alert Bay, British Columbia. She also told me about the day her small boat was lost in the fog and several orcas she knew showed up and led her safely home.

Ken Balcomb has an almost identical story about being saved by a pod of the orcas he studied.

The Nuu-chah-nulth people in Washington State say the spirits of their dead chiefs can transfer to orcas.

The Kwakw<u>a</u>ka'wakw in BC say the first human beings were orcas. The orcas came onto land, became people and forgot to return home.

Meet one of the smallest orca ecotypes—a type B2 (Gerlache) orca. Scientists think they specialize in hunting penguins. Their yellow tint is caused by algae. JOSH MCINNES

The Haida in northern BC and Alaska say orcas show up for funerals. Indigenous stories used to be dismissed by non-Indigenous people as myths or legends, which makes it tough to explain why orcas keep showing up at Haida funerals. Just before writer Stephen Reid died on Haida Gwaii in 2018, seven orcas appeared in the water nearby. His wife, poet Susan Musgrave, was sure they'd shown up to send him off.

When Michael Bigg's ashes were scattered in Johnstone Strait, thirty orcas arrived to witness the ceremony.

Between 2011 and 2018 there have been six gatherings of orca lovers in Friday Harbor on San Juan Island. Each of these conventions is called Superpod in honor of the whales' getting together. San Juan Island is one of the best places in the world to watch orcas, but the southern residents haven't been around much over the last few years. You can certainly never count on them showing up. Except for Superpod. When J pod arrived on the first day of the 2018 event, people were happy but not surprised. On the final night, the Superpod people (including me) partied in Lime Kiln Point Park, and members of J pod showed up like they'd been invited. They've appeared at all six gatherings of the humans devoted to helping them.

The night I decided to read part of this book to an audience for the first time ever, something impossible happened. I'd been invited to talk in the park at East Point on Saturna Island. I was sitting on the grass in almost the exact spot where Joe Bauer and Sam Burich camped years ago as they waited to harpoon a whale. A few minutes before my talk, someone shouted, "Whale!"—just like Joe Bauer did back when he saw Moby Doll in 1964. But it wasn't just a whale,

Princess Angeline, Kiki and Moby racing down Boundary Pass in the Salish Sea. TASLI SHAW

it was J pod—Moby's family. This was the first time I'd ever seen them from the shores of Saturna. And they weren't just swimming; they were breaching over and over and over, in the same spot where Moby was captured. For almost half an hour everyone in the park watched the whales play. A few minutes after the whales swam off, I read the audience this chapter—except for this new paragraph:

In Shakespeare's play *Hamlet*, the prince tells his pal, Horatio, "There are more things in heaven and earth, Horatio, than are dreamt of in your philosophy." Orcas continually prove there are more things in the ocean than are dreamt of in our science.

An orca calf leaps beside its mother.
DAVE ELLIFRIT/NATIONAL OCEANIC AND ATMOSPHERIC ADMINISTRATION/DEPARTMENT OF COMMERCE

A male orca off the coast of
Skjervøy, Norway.
ALESSANDRO DE MADDALENA

15

Orcas Everywhere

"Where whales journey,
people follow."

—Maori wisdom

Orcas on the hunt for herring near a fishing boat in Kaldfjord, Norway.
ALESSANDRO DE MADDALENA

There's only one mammal that shows up in more places on the planet than orcas. You guessed it—humans. Orcas are in every ocean. And each orca culture is unique. Researchers in Switzerland released a study in 2016 showing that orcas are the only animal on the planet besides humans who evolved on the basis of culture. They found that whales in different parts of the world became biologically distinct and developed different diets and behaviors based on their surroundings.

When Michael Bigg realized there were two types of orcas in the Salish Sea, he'd only hit the tip of the orca iceberg. In 1979 researchers spotted a group of orcas with terrible teeth and scarred skin. About a decade later scientists realized the orcas' teeth were worn down and the animals were covered with battle scars because of their diet. The sleeper sharks they eat have very rough skin—like sandpaper. This group of orcas—called *offshores* because they hang out in the open ocean—was an all-new group to us, with their own look and culture.

Humans display their traditional cultures with costumes, art, dance, music and food. Orca clans can't dress up. Maybe their moves and sounds aren't dance or music. But maybe they are. Their diets, traditions and dialects are arguably more distinct from place to place than ours are. After all, orcas everywhere aren't all drinking Starbucks coffee, listening to Drake and watching *YouTube*.

It's not easy for scientists to declare there's a new species out there. For the most part, species are still based on categories Linnaeus came up with. And the rules are complicated. They require scientists to review a dead specimen that can be used as a perfect symbol of the species.

This isn't an easy thing to do with an orca. So instead of separating orcas into different species, the word scientists use is *ecotypes*.

There appear to be at least ten distinct orca ecotypes:

Residents are fish-eating orcas and can be found all along the shorelines of the Pacific Ocean. They live in close-knit family groups, and each pod has its own dialect.

Bigg's whales live on the Pacific Coast, hunt in smaller groups than residents do and hunt quietly. This is so their prey can't hear them coming. Orcas elsewhere—such as in Russia—also separate along the same lines as fish eaters and mammal eaters.

Offshores are shark eaters (sleepers, blues and salmon sharks), although they have been seen eating halibut. They're smaller than residents and Bigg's whales, their teeth wear down quickly, and they hang out in the North Pacific Ocean.

Type 1 Eastern North Atlantic orcas live near Norway, Iceland and Scotland; they are closer in size to dolphins and less fussy about food.

Type 2 Eastern North Atlantic orcas are the mammal eaters who likely earned orcas their fierce reputation. They are larger than most other orcas and have black masklike eye patches and worn-down teeth.

Antarctic Type A orcas (Southern Hemisphere) are big whales—up to 31 feet (9.5 meters)—who use their size and speed to catch bigger whales, especially minkes.

Pack ice orcas (also known as Type B) hunt seals in the pack ice around the Antarctic. They are famous for making waves, using their bodies to splash seals off ice floes and into the water. The skin of these whales sometimes looks brown or yellow, and they're paler than your average orca.

ORCA BITES

Ecotypes

Ecotype basically means "species"—although without the official scientific seal of approval. Orca ecotypes look, act and speak differently from one another, and they haven't bred with one another in more than half a million years.

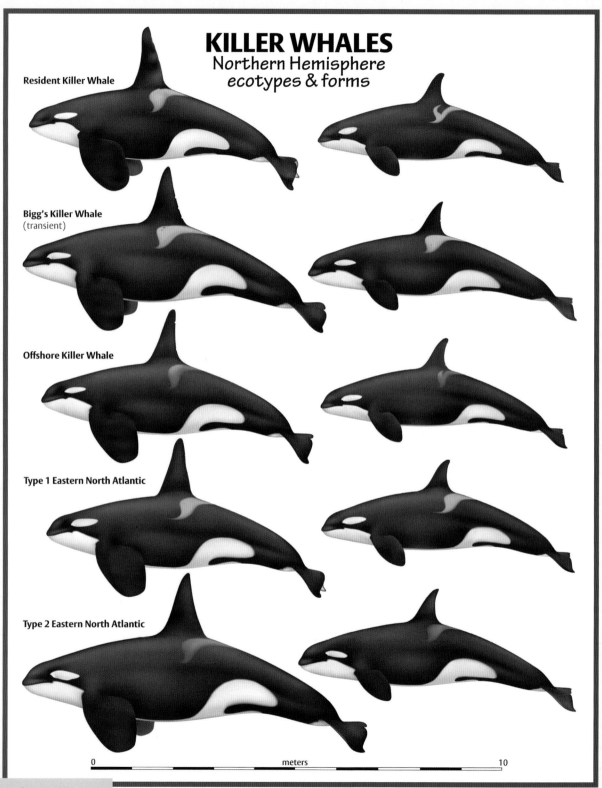

KILLER WHALES
Northern Hemisphere
ecotypes & forms

Resident Killer Whale

Bigg's Killer Whale
(transient)

Offshore Killer Whale

Type 1 Eastern North Atlantic

Type 2 Eastern North Atlantic

0   meters   10

Orcas of the world.
UKO GORTER

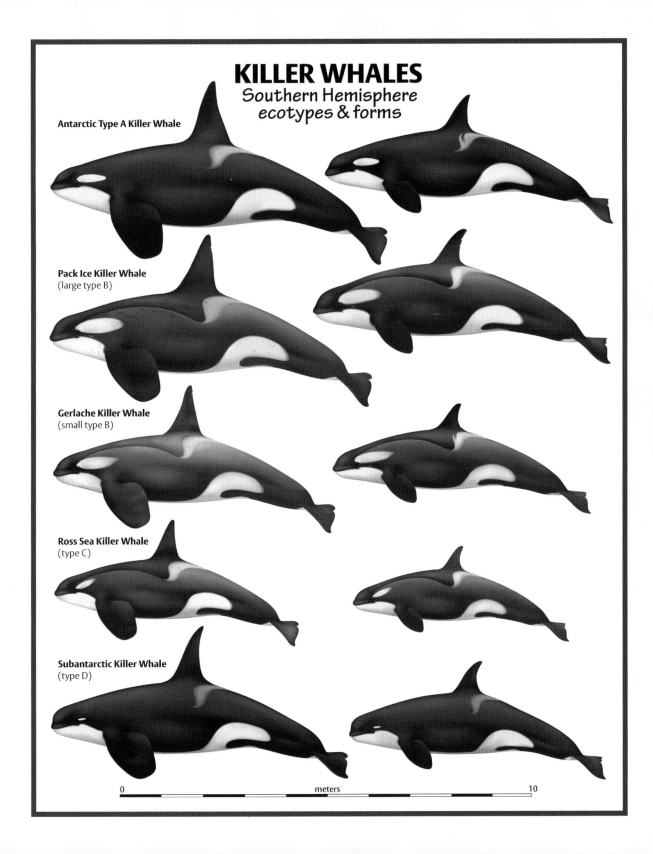

KILLER WHALES
Southern Hemisphere ecotypes & forms

Antarctic Type A Killer Whale

Pack Ice Killer Whale
(large type B)

Gerlache Killer Whale
(small type B)

Ross Sea Killer Whale
(type C)

Subantarctic Killer Whale
(type D)

0   meters   10

Gerlache orcas, also known as Type B (small), are fans of picnicking on penguins. These orcas look like pack ice orcas and have the same coloring but are smaller.

Ross Sea orcas, also known as Type C, look like big dolphins. The largest males grow to only 20 feet (6 meters). They are closer to gray and yellow than black and white. These orcas eat toothfish, but we're not sure how many other things they feed on.

Subantarctic orcas, also known as Type D, were first identified in 1955 when a group beached in New Zealand. These mammal eaters have sharp dorsals—like those of Bigg's whales—and the smallest white eye patches of any orcas. They also have rounder heads. In 2018 researchers saw a pod hunting seals in Antarctica. Ds also like toothfish.

New Zealand orcas have been studied mostly by a single researcher, Dr. Ingrid Visser. She's identified three local types (they may not be distinct ecotypes). The orcas she's studied eat sharks and dolphins, and work in teams to catch stingrays. They dig them up, pin them down and pluck their stingers in shallow water.

Russia appears to have the same two ecotypes as the Salish Sea—fish eaters (lovers of salmon and mackerel) and mammal eaters (who like minke).

No one has decided yet whether the orcas who live near Britain, Hawaii or the Gulf of Mexico are genetically unique, but every pod seems to be culturally unique.

FINDING FAMILY

Onyx

Male southern resident orcas spend their lives with their moms. When she dies, they tend not to live much longer. But some male whales are different. Onyx (L87) was

The killer whales used a technique called wave washing to dislodge seals from pack ice.
ROBERT PITMAN/NATIONAL OCEANIC AND ATMOSPHERIC ADMINISTRATION/DEPARTMENT OF COMMERCE

born in 1992 and lost his mom, Olympia (L32), in 2005. He left his family to join K-pod matriarchs Lummi (K7) and Georgia (K11). When Lummi died two years later, Onyx stayed with Georgia. When she died in 2010, he joined J pod and became inseparable from Granny (J2). When Granny died he stuck with J pod, and the last time I checked he was either hanging out with some of the guys or following Tahlequah (J35).

Putita

Putita (NZ126), an orca who lives near Tutukaka, New Zealand, is also famous for moving from pod to pod. He was stranded and rescued twice by people. When he was stranded in 2011 after chasing stingrays too close to shore, his mom, Yin, and big brother Rua hung out nearby, waiting for humans to help him out.

Onyx and Granny.
VAL SHORE

Meeting Skana at the Vancouver Aquarium. REX WEYLER/GREENPEACE

16

Tanks for the Memories

"No aquarium, no tank in a marine land, however spacious it may be, can begin to duplicate the conditions of the sea. And no dolphin who inhabits one of those aquariums or one of those marine lands can be considered normal."

—Jacques-Yves Cousteau, explorer

ORCA BITES

Whale watching

There are all sorts of ways to watch and listen to orcas in the wild.

Wherever there are whales, there are usually whale-watching boats. Like any other boats, large or small, these can interfere with orcas' sleeping, eating and mating. Professional whale watchers are likely to follow laws that protect the whales. These laws spell out how far away from the orcas the boats have to stay, when motors can and can't be used, and proper behavior around wildlife.

If you're thinking about taking a whale-watching tour, do your research to see which companies work with whale-protection groups. The most trustworthy whale-watching companies often work for or with researchers.

The most famous orcas in the world are or were on display in tanks.

These are the orcas most humans have met.

In many cases—like mine—these are the first whales we fell in love with.

Once upon a time these were the only whales we knew how to study. But today almost the only thing we learn from studying orcas in captivity is how orcas react to captivity.

Attitudes toward orcas vary between countries and cultures.

In North America catching whales to display has been taboo since the 1970s. But it is only since the backlash caused by the documentary *Blackfish* (for more about *Blackfish*, see chapter 17) that SeaWorld—the most active orca exhibitor in the world—agreed to stop breeding orcas for display.

In Russia orcas are still caught for display in marine parks (mostly in China). The Far East Russia Orca Project is leading the fight against this new wave of captures in the Okhotsk Sea.

Thanks to anti-captivity activists—and movies like *Free Willy* and *Blackfish*—people aren't still catching orcas for display in North America (and that fight is shifting to other cetaceans, including belugas and dolphins). Meanwhile, cetacean champions like Lori Marino (who proved dolphins can conquer the mirror test) are working to create seaside sanctuaries. These refuges would allow captive cetaceans to live in a more natural environment.

Some people want to send all captive whales "home," but for most North American orcas in aquariums, the only home they've ever known is a tank. As of 2018 there were twenty-one orcas in SeaWorld's North American parks.

All but three were born in captivity. In some cases these captive orcas are the result of interbreeding between ecotypes who have not bred with each other in the wild for more than half a million years.

LOLITA AND CORKY

The only two North American captive orcas who were born in the oceans are Lolita and Corky.

Lolita still recognizes the calls of her family. Because names have power, people fighting for Lolita's release often call her Tokitae—a Chinook term meaning "nice day, pretty colors." It sounds as if it was given to her by an Indigenous community. It wasn't. Tokitae was the first name someone from SeaWorld came up with for her after seeing the word in a gift shop. A few days later someone else at SeaWorld renamed her Lolita.

The Lummi Nation delivers a totem to Tokitae. SACREDSEA.ORG

ORCA BITES

Land-based whale watching

The best way to watch the whales without disturbing them is from the land. In North America there is a "whale trail"—a list of spots where orcas regularly swim close enough to shore that you can see them. One of those spots is East Point on Saturna Island, where Moby Doll was harpooned.

If you like to listen to orcas, there are websites sharing live whale sounds from around the world. I've listed some at the back of this book.

Today Tokitae has been adopted as the orca's name by the Lummi people. In 2012 a Washington State ferry was named *Tokitae* in her honor.

Corky (actually Corky II—an earlier captive named Corky died in 1971) is a member of the northern resident A5 pod. She was caught in the Salish Sea in 1969 and is the longest-lived captive orca. In 1993 Corky shuddered when she heard a recording of A5 pod's calls.

She was the first orca to give birth in captivity, which she did a half dozen times. None of her calves lived longer than forty-eight days. Paul Spong is a passionate campaigner for Corky's return to British Columbia waters.

MIRACLE

In 1977 a baby whale was seen swimming in Menzies Bay near Campbell River, BC, and appeared separated from her family. She had been shot. Fisherman Bill Davis saw the dying young orca and began feeding her by hand. The Vancouver Aquarium and Sealand of the Pacific in Victoria, BC, caught the whale and transported

An injured Miracle being checked out by veterinarians and others in the outdoor saltwater pool at the Oak Bay Beach Hotel in Victoria, BC.
ROCHELLE TERMEHR

her to Sealand on a flat deck truck. A team of veterinarians nursed her back to health but she became the center of a major battle over captivity. Should she be returned to the ocean or was she too accustomed to humans to survive in the wild? We never found out. In 1982 Miracle died at Sealand. Did she die in an attempt to set her free or did she die due to her captivity? It's a mystery explored in a 2009 movie called *Who Killed Miracle?*

MORGAN

In 2010 a starving orca was swimming off the coast of the Netherlands, and the Dolfinarium Harderwijk received a permit for "rescue, rehabilitation and release." The Dolfinarium named the orca Morgan, trained her and kept her in a tiny tank for almost two years. When animal rights groups challenged the Dutch government and the park, they sent Morgan to the Loro Parque Aquarium in Spain. Orca lovers around the world formed the Free Morgan Foundation to fight to send her back to her family in Norway. As of this writing, Morgan is still in captivity.

ORCA BITES

In captivity

In 2018 there were 60 captive orcas in 14 marine parks in the United States, Canada, France, Spain, Japan, Russia and China.

Morgan in the tank in Spain.
FREE MORGAN.ORG

WHO KILLED MIRACLE?
a documentary

everyone loved the baby killer whale called Miracle. five years after her daring rescue, she was found dead. who was responsible?

Gordon Green from the Royal BC Museum swimming with Miracle at Sealand of the Pacific in Victoria, BC.
BRENT COOKE

the truth may break your heart.

17

Orca Celebrities

"We live in a media culture. A political statement in a feature movie will do more than all the educational efforts of all the environmental groups combined."

—Captain Paul Watson, founder, Sea Shepherd Conservation Society

I called Moby Doll "The Killer Whale Who Changed the World" because he helped convince humans that orcas weren't monsters. Skana inspired Greenpeace. Miracle helped prove orcas in the wild can be rescued. Here are a few other orca superstars who have made major waves.

KEIKO

Keiko became world famous for playing the starring cetacean role in the 1993 movie *Free Willy*. The movie ends, as many classic animal stories do, with the captive being set free. But the image of Willy flying over his aquarium wall captured the world's imagination. So did the story of the real whale who played Willy, who lived in worse conditions than the imaginary orca.

Keiko was caught in Iceland in 1979 as a baby. He was displayed in an amusement park in Mexico City. Keiko's pool was much smaller than the pools most orcas were kept in, and the water was far too hot for an orca from Iceland. When filmmakers arrived in 1992 to make their movie, Keiko was thin and had a nasty skin condition. This was bad for Keiko but great for the movie. The movie was a hit, and the world fell in love with Willy (and Keiko). Millions of dollars were donated to the Free Willy-Keiko Foundation. And it was children who led the fight to free the orca.

In 1996 Keiko was moved from Mexico to a much nicer aquarium in Newport, Oregon. He soon gained more than 1,000 pounds (454 kilograms). Newport was supposed to be a brief stop on his way home, but the aquarium managers wanted to keep their new star.

After two years of protests from orca lovers around the world, Keiko was finally flown home to Iceland in 1998. Icelandic orcas aren't well studied, so no one knew how to

Keiko, the orca who played Willy in the movie *Free Willy*, in his tank in Oregon before being flown home to Iceland.
US DEPARTMENT OF DEFENSE

find Keiko's family. The orca who had spent his life eating dead fish and surrounded by humans had to learn how to hunt and eat live fish. And he didn't want to leave the humans who were there to help him find his home. Keiko finally swam to Norway, where he looked for humans and let children ride on him.

Keiko may have returned to the wild, but he never found his family. He died of pneumonia after five years of being monitored in the ocean.

LUNA

This southern resident orca had multiple identities in the human world. His scientific designation was L98, but he was named Luna after a Seattle newspaper held a whale-naming contest. The name was chosen to suggest that an orca "explores the ocean like the moon explores the earth." Young male orcas rarely leave their mom's side, and when this orca lost his mom, he adopted the humans of Nootka Sound on Vancouver Island.

When Luna started playing with people and boats, humans couldn't agree on how to deal with him. Many people living in Nootka Sound—and tourists—loved having a playful orca around. But some worried he'd damage their boats or interfere with their fishing.

Luna didn't just hang out; he came so close to people that they could—and did—pet him. Some people wanted to catch him and return him to his family. Some wanted to do whatever it took to get him out of Nootka Sound. But the Mowachaht/Muchalaht First Nations said the whale was their former chief. The orca appeared in the harbor just days after Ambrose Maquinna died, so they named the orca Tsu'xiit in his honor.

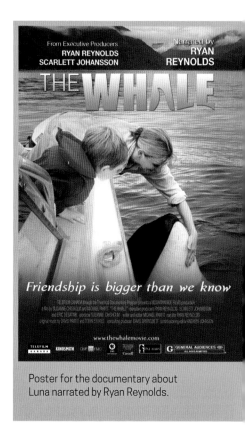

Poster for the documentary about Luna narrated by Ryan Reynolds.

The curious young orca was six years old when a tugboat ran into him.

His story is told in the 2011 documentary film *The Whale*, narrated by Ryan Reynolds.

MAGA

In a story about Maga's hunting moves, a journalist wondered if she was the Thomas Edison of orcas. Edison invented the lightbulb (and hundreds of other things). This matriarch of a mammal-eating pod off the coast of Argentina keeps inventing new ways to hunt.

Maga (which means "magician") leads the only orcas known to hunt on land. She teaches members of her pod to throw themselves onto the beach in Patagonia, capture baby sea lions and roll back into the sea on the next wave. She works with another orca, Jazmin, to hunt dolphins

Orcas who hunt on the land off the coast of Argentina.
FOTO4440/SHUTTERSTOCK.COM

with all-new moves. The pod spots dolphins, and then Maga splits off. The other members of the pod herd the dolphins toward their matriarch. When the dolphins find Maga waiting for them, it's too late.

Maga head-butts a shocked dolphin—a knockout move. Then she throws the stunned dolphin into the air to kill it, and her pod has dolphin for dinner.

Maga's family is featured in the 2016 movie *The Lighthouse of the Orcas*.

TILIKUM

The star of the 2013 anti-captivity documentary *Blackfish* was the first killer whale to truly live up to the ancient image of a killer whale as a killer of humans. Originally from Iceland, Tilikum was kept in a small tank in Sealand of the Pacific in Victoria, BC, with two other orcas.

Tilikum performing a Shamu show in SeaWorld in Florida.
DAVID R. TRIBBLE/CC BY-SA 3.0.

The whale who went home

Springer (A73) was born right at the beginning 2000, but she wasn't famous for being the northern residents' millennium baby. When her mother died in 2002, Springer was swimming alone in Puget Sound, Washington, approaching humans to say hi. She was clearly a sick whale. She had bad breath and bad skin and was infected by worms. Since capture had been banned years earlier, humans weren't sure what to do. After much debate Canadian and US government agencies agreed to capture her. She was taken into captivity for food and medical treatment. Six months later she was taken home to her pod. Not only did her family take her back, but as of 2017 she'd had two babies in the wild.

At night he was kept in a space so small it would have been almost impossible to sleep.

One afternoon, in front of a crowd of tourists, twenty-year-old trainer Keltie Byrne fell into the pool. The coroner reported that Tilikum and the other two orcas in the pool kept her under water until she drowned.

SeaWorld bought the whale, and Tilikum was flown to Orlando, Florida. He soon dragged another trainer, Dawn Brancheau, into the water and killed her. He also killed a visitor who broke into into the park when it was closed.

The killer killer whale was still the star of SeaWorld's breeding program. He fathered most orcas born there and died in 2017.

Blackfish sparked the sea change in North America that led to SeaWorld agreeing to end breeding and stop showing orcas in captivity. Eventually, Tilikum's story finished what Moby Doll's started—ending the business of catching and displaying orcas in North America.

SCARLET

When researchers first saw a new baby whale in December 2015, they were thrilled to greet the first new arrival in two years. Then they got closer to the newborn and discovered that she really was a miracle baby. Her body was covered with scars because the mother, Slick (J16), wasn't able to give birth without help. So at least one other orca gently held the baby with her teeth and pulled Scarlet (J50) free from her mom, saving both mother and calf.

Three years later Scarlet was seen looking very hungry. We know orcas are starving when the blubber at the back of their heads disappears, causing an indentation. This is called peanut head, and it usually means a whale is close to death. The US and Canadian governments, the Lummi Nation and nearly a dozen other groups joined forces to give her medicine and save her life. They failed. She died in September 2018, and her death sparked an outcry for action to save the southern residents before it's too late.

Scarlet and Slick on the hunt for Chinook salmon. NATIONAL OCEANIC AND ATMOSPHERIC ADMINISTRATION/ DEPARTMENT OF COMMERCE

Artist Ted Harrison's 1988 painting
Orca. COURTESY TED HARRISON ESTATE

18

Orcas and You

"All whales matter.
All cetaceans matter.
All life matters."

—Elizabeth May, leader, Green Party of Canada

Puffin is one of the last remaining females in Scotland's vanishing West Coast Community. HEBRIDEAN WHALE AND DOLPHIN TRUST

In the spring 2019, the population of southern residents has fallen to seventy-five orcas. Their official status in America is *endangered*. In order for them to leave the endangered list, their population would have to more than double to 155. Other orca populations around the world are endangered.

Some orca clans are already doomed to extinction. The Bigg's AT1 pod and resident AB pods in Alaska never recovered—and never will—from deaths caused by an oil spill in 1989. There are no females left, so there will be no new babies.

The orca clan near Scotland was down to eight as of 2018—four males and four females. The males are John Coe, Comet, Floppy Fin and Aquarius. The females are Nicola, Moneypenny, Puffin and Occasus. No new babies have been born to the pod, known as the West Coast Community, in more than twenty years. When former podmate Lulu washed up on the shore of Tiree in 2016, scientists found more toxins in her body than humans had discovered in almost any marine mammal in history. The chemicals included PCBS—polychlorinated biphenyls—which were used in electronic equipment until the 1970s. One effect of PCBS is that they destroy an animal's reproductive system.

As always, the only real threat to orcas is us.

When I ask scientists what to tell people who wonder why they should care about orcas, the answer I hear most often is that orcas are the "canaries in the coal mine." Miners used to test for poison gas by carrying caged canaries into mine shafts. Since canaries have tiny lungs, they can't last long in a poisonous environment. If the canary died, the humans got out.

Scientists warn that if orcas can't survive, we won't either.

WHAT CAN WE DO TO HELP ORCAS?

The biggest threats to orcas vary from whale to whale and ocean to ocean, but here are ten things we can do to help save the whales, the oceans and ourselves.

1. Stop throwing so much stuff "away."

Humans make a big mess. North Americans are traditionally the winners when it comes to creating garbage. All garbage goes somewhere. Spoiler alert: This mystical land of Away where we throw things? It's our oceans. The less trash we create, the better world we're making for the whales—and humans.

Some countries have leftover land mines from wars. Orcas face a similar danger known as "ghost gear"—fishing nets that were cut loose as trash. Humans abandon 706,479 tons (640,000 tonnes) of fishing equipment to the ocean every year, including nets the size of football fields.

We also dump too many toxins into the water. Chemicals humans stopped using decades ago are still in the ocean. Fish are full of human medicine. Medicine needs to be properly disposed of. So do paints.

Pesticides that kill bugs end up in the water eventually.

Sunscreens are poisoning coral reefs. If we can't eat these chemicals, neither can zooplankton or fish or orcas.

Think about what you eat, what you use and what will end up in the oceans.

2. Pass on plastic.

When I was a kid we used to worry about nuclear waste, because there's no safe way to get rid of it. Meanwhile, everything everywhere in my world was being replaced by plastic, and almost everyone thought that was awesome. Nobody seemed to give a second thought to the fact that there's no way to dispose of plastic either.

Seal caught in fishing nets.
IAN DYBALL/ISTOCK.COM

Whale on the menu

When I visited Norway a few years ago, I asked a woman in her early 20s if she liked whales. Her answer was yes. Then she explained: "Seared. With lingonberry sauce." In Norway and Finland, people still have minke on the menu—and whale used to be on a lot of menus in other countries too. In North America in the 1950s, diced whale loin with added gravy was sold in stores. The cans came with recipes for meat pie, curried whale and whale stew.

Plastic is everywhere. When it breaks down into small enough pieces, it ends up in our food and water. Plastic is now a toxic link in the food chain. There will soon be more plastic in the ocean than zooplankton.

There are *gyres*—swirling islands of plastics that are the size of large countries—in every ocean. If we don't clean up our act by 2050, plastic in the ocean will outweigh the fish because of overfishing and overpolluting. Whales and other species are dying after eating plastic instead of food. In 2018 a sperm whale's body was found on the shore with more than 60 pounds (27.2 kilograms) of plastic in his stomach.

Whenever you can, say no to single-use plastic. Do you really need that straw? Do you really need that plastic bag or fork or cup or…?

Reduce. Reuse. Recycle. Repeat.

3. Consider climate change.

Some people say climate change isn't caused by humans. These people are almost never scientists. Most scientists are freaking out over climate change and the impact it's having on our oceans. It's leading to *ocean acidification*—a condition caused by excess carbon dioxide turning water more acidic, which kills sea life like coral and zooplankton.

Find out what you can do in your community to combat climate change.

4. Quiet down.

We're loud, and so are our boats.

Orcas communicate primarily through sound and sonar. That's also how they hunt. For orcas to survive and thrive, we need to limit the sounds boats are sinking into our oceans.

5. Get orcas off the menu.

Orcas aren't popular as meals, but some people still consider them food.

Japanese are eating the masters of the open seas. So are some people in the Caribbean. Inuit in Greenland used to rely on other species for food, but now that their water is heating up, some of those species have vanished and orcas are available. They say orcas taste just like narwhal.

This isn't a big threat to orcas. Yet. But climate change means orcas are showing up in new places and fish that used to be eaten are vanishing.

And starving people will eat anything that's out there.

We need to make sure we're keeping orcas off dinner plates everywhere. And shaming people doesn't work if we're not helping to feed them.

6. Share the resources.

Humans like to claim we're the only beings on the planet who are altruistic, but, unlike orcas, we don't always share our food. In the Salish Sea, southern residents are starving because there isn't enough Chinook salmon to go around.

In places like Tasmania, Alaska and northern British Columbia, orcas are chasing fishing boats to fight for food—a battle likely to end with fishermen going back to carrying rifles to shoot their rivals.

7. Think globally, act locally.

Every community everywhere has environmental groups dealing with issues that affect our oceans. Find the issue that speaks to you and get involved.

You can make a difference.

Minke on the menu in Norway.
MARK LEIREN-YOUNG

8. Get political.

Most politicians want people to love them. It doesn't matter how old you are—if you speak up about issues you can make a difference. Children led the fight to free Keiko. You can write letters, make calls, volunteer for causes that matter to you or start your own movement.

In Canada thirteen-year-old Simon Jackson helped lead the fight to save the Kermode bears (a type of black bear) also known as spirit bears. Autumn Peltier was thirteen when she told the United Nations about the importance of protecting the water. Ta'Kaiya Blaney spoke to the United Nations about environmental issues five times before she was sixteen.

Eight-year-old Kady McKenna led the fight to recycle electronics in Florida. Eight-year-old Paloma Russ helped raise money and awareness to save endangered cheetahs. Robbie Bond was eight when he helped launch a group to save the nation's parks. There are young eco-heroes around the world. You can join them.

9. Spread the word.

If you think something is important, share the news. Share your ideas and concerns. Tell your family. Tell your friends. Write about them. Passion makes a difference. Passion inspires people.

Some people will try to shut you down no matter what you say. It's the nature of the real world and the virtual one. They can tell their stories; stay true to yours.

10. Agree that orcas are persons too.

If an orca had the same rights as a human, we'd have to share the fish and the oceans and stop dumping our trash into their homes. Saving the orcas means saving ourselves.

Mark Leiren-Young with Tahlequah and her daughter outside the British Columbia Parliament Buildings. RAYNE ELLYCRYS BENU

If we discovered orcas on another planet, there's no doubt we'd celebrate finding intelligent life.

So why don't orcas have rights?

I don't think the answer has anything to do with what's right or wrong or legal. It's all about claiming that the planet—and everything on it—belongs to humans.

Imagine if we had to share our oceans and our resources.

Imagine if we had to share our world.

Imagine how much more amazing our world would be.

Orca in Motion, painting by Tasli Shaw.

ELLA

At eight years old Canadian Ella Grace launched a campaign
called Ella Saves the Ocean and started cleaning up beaches,
inspiring others to do the same. KATE GRACE

"I want to be part of the generation that goes down in history as the ones who stopped using animals for entertainment. The ones who realized that captivity is no life for a wild animal. I want to be the generation that my great-grandchildren look back on with pride, because we finally stopped acting like the planet was here as our trash bin, and we finally realized that we share this planet equally with animals. I want to be part of the generation that can apologize for all the senseless cruelty, and stops the destruction of our beautiful oceans. I want to be the generation that sees that the world is bigger than just me."

RIDHIMA

At age nine Ridhima Choudhary sued the Indian government for
not doing enough to fight climate change. FINISH PANDEY

"Children of today and the future will disproportionately suffer the dangers and catastrophic impacts of climate destabilization and ocean acidification. I can realize that the situation is getting bleak, with a lot of deforestation in the name of development, reduction in funding for conservation-based projects and non-implementation of all the laws pertaining to environment. This makes me worried about the future for us children."

ROBBIE

When he was nine years old, Robbie Bond launched Kids
Speak for Parks to fight for parkland in America.
ALANA EAGLE

"You are never too young to take action for the environment.
Your voice matters, and there are many different ways you can
protect the environment: for example, reducing your single-use
plastic. There are so many organizations and people who are
happy to help you along the way!"

LONDON

London Fletcher of Washington State began speaking to governments
to fight for orcas and salmon when she was nine.
JOEL FLETCHER

"When the federal government listed our orcas as endangered under the Endangered Species Act, it made a promise—a promise to protect them and to do everything in its power to preserve them. A promise to preserve their habitat and a promise that future generations such as my own will be able to look out over the water and have a chance to see this national treasure in their own habitat swimming freely, without fear of starving to death, or having their calls drowned out by our ever-increasing marine traffic. They are free beings, but they are at the mercy of corporate greed."

DECLARATION OF RIGHTS FOR CETACEANS: WHALES AND DOLPHINS

Agreed, 22nd May 2010, Helsinki, Finland

Based on the principle of the equal treatment of all persons;

Recognizing that scientific research gives us deeper insights into the complexities of cetacean minds, societies and cultures;

Noting that the progressive development of international law manifests an entitlement to life by cetaceans;

We *affirm* that all cetaceans as persons have the right to life, liberty and wellbeing.

We conclude that:

1. Every individual cetacean has the right to life.

2. No cetacean should be held in captivity or servitude; be subject to cruel treatment; or be removed from their natural environment.

3. All cetaceans have the right to freedom of movement and residence within their natural environment.

4. No cetacean is the property of any State, corporation, human group or individual.

5. Cetaceans have the right to the protection of their natural environment.

6. Cetaceans have the right not to be subject to the disruption of their cultures.

7. The rights, freedoms and norms set forth in this Declaration should be protected under international and domestic law.

8. Cetaceans are entitled to an international order in which these rights, freedoms and norms can be fully realized.

9. No State, corporation, human group or individual should engage in any activity that undermines these rights, freedoms and norms.

10. Nothing in this Declaration shall prevent a State from enacting stricter provisions for the protection of cetacean rights.

Rayne Ellycrys Benu and Mark Leiren-Young waiting for the whales on a beach in BC. KRIS KRÜG

GLOSSARY

albino—a person or animal without pigment in their skin, hair and eyes

altruism—selfless concern for others

anthropocentrism—the belief that humans are the rock stars of all living things

anthropodenial—a word invented by animal researcher Frans de Waal that means "a blindness to the humanlike characteristics of other animals or the animal-like characteristics of ourselves."

anthropology—the study of human societies

anthropomorphizing—thinking a god, animal or thing has emotions or experiences similar to ours

apex predator—a predator at the top of a food chain

baleen—a filter-feeding system inside the mouths of baleen whales

Bigg's whales—mammal-eating orcas in the Salish Sea named after Michael Bigg, the Canadian scientist who discovered that there are different types of orcas

biosonar—sonar that's biological—part of an animal's wiring—and not technological (see echolocation)

botanist—someone who makes a scientific study of plants

breach—a whale's leap out of the ocean and into the air

cetacean—the Latin word for members of the whale family

collagen—protein that holds a body together, like biological glue

commercial whaling—catching and killing whales to sell their body parts

dialect—a set of calls, or songs in the case of birds, that is unique to areas, populations or social groups. Some scientists prefer the term *language*.

dorsal—the fin on an orca's back; *dorsal* means "back"

echolocation—the use of sound waves (or sonar) to locate, find or identify something by the way the sound echoes (or bounces) off the target

empirical data—information acquired by observation or experimentation

food chain—a series of living things that are linked to each other because each feeds on the next

geoglyph—an image made of carefully arranged stones

gyres—large systems of rotating ocean currents; now often used to refer to swirling islands of plastic waste in the ocean

industrial whaling—catching and killing huge numbers of whales to sell their body parts

keratin—a strong natural protein that forms hair, nails, hoofs, horns, feathers, etc.

matriarchal—led by a matriarch, which in orca society is the oldest female and leader of the pod or pods

melanin—pigment that adds color to skin, hair and eyes

mirror self-recognition—a test based on the theory that if an animal can recognize itself in the mirror, then it is "self-aware"

northern residents—resident orcas who range from Alaska to BC

ocean acidification—when ocean water turns acidic—and poisonous—due to chemicals and climate change

offshores—orcas in the Pacific Ocean whose primary food is sleeper sharks

PCBs—synthetic industrial chemicals toxic to orcas and pretty much everything else on the planet

petroglyph—an image drawn or carved into stone

pod—a whale community, so named because fishermen used to say whales stayed together "like peas in a pod."

rorqual—any of the large baleen whales that have relatively small heads, short, broad plates of baleen, and deep furrows on the skin

saddle patch—the distinct marking on the back of an orca

Salish Sea—the waterways in the Pacific Ocean along the coast of southern British Columbia and northern Washington State

southern residents—the famous fish-eating orcas who live primarily in the Salish Sea

sonar—a method of detecting, locating and determining the speed or size of objects through the use of reflected sound waves

spindle neurons—the cells in the brain that process emotions

sprouter—a teenage male orca whose dorsal fin has suddenly grown or sprouted

spy-hopping—whales or other marine mammals poking their heads out of the water to check out what's happening on the surface

superpod—a large gathering of whales

taxonomy—rules scientists use for categorizing living things

vocalizations—the sounds an orca makes

zooplankton—super-tiny fish like krill that float rather than swim and are the fave food of baleen whales

RESOURCES

VIDEO AND AUDIO

Watch Wild Orcas

Center for Whale Research: youtube.com/user/center4whaleresearch

Listen to Wild Orcas

Lime Kiln Hydrophone:
smruconsulting.com/products-tools/lime-kiln-live-hydrophone/
Orcasound: orcasound.net/listen/
The Right Whale Listening Network: listenforwhales.org

ORCA MOVIES

Blackfish
Free Willy
Killers of Eden
The Hundred-Year-Old Whale
The Killer Whale Who Changed the World
The Whale
Who Killed Miracle?

RELATED WEBSITES

Action for Nature: actionfornature.org
American Cetacean Society: acsonline.org
Be Whale Wise: bewhalewise.org
Center for Whale Research: whaleresearch.com
David Suzuki Foundation: davidsuzuki.org
Department of Fisheries and Oceans (Canada): dfo-mpo.gc.ca
Eden Killer Whale Museum: killerwhalemuseum.com.au
Free Morgan Foundation: freemorgan.org
Killer Whale Tales: killerwhaletales.org
Kimmela Center for Animal Advocacy: kimmela.org
Nonhuman Rights Project: nonhumanrightsproject.org

Ocean Futures Society: oceanfutures.org

OrcaLab: orcalab.org/about

Orca Network: orcanetwork.org

Russian Orcas Homepage: russianorca.com/project.php?lang=en

Saturna Heritage Centre: saturnaheritage.ca

Saving the Southern Residents (NOAA): https://bit.ly/2IDI9P2

Save Our Wild Salmon: wildsalmon.org

SeaDoc Society: seadocsociety.org

Sea Shepherd Conservation Society: seashepherd.org

Vancouver Aquarium: vanaqua.org

WDC (Whale and Dolphin Conservation): us.whales.org

Whale Museum (Friday Harbor, WA): whalemuseum.org

The Whale Trail: thewhaletrail.org

Wild Whales—B.C. Cetacean Sightings Network: wildwhales.org

BOOKS

Colby, Jason. *Orcas: How We Came to Know and Love the Ocean's Greatest Predator.* New York, NY: Oxford University Press, 2018.

Ford, John K.B., Graeme M. Ellis and Kenneth C. Balcomb. *Killer Whales: The Natural History and Genealogy of* Orcinus orca *in British Columbia and Washington State.* Vancouver, BC: University of British Columbia Press, 1999 (updated edition).

Hoyt, Erich. *Encyclopedia of Whales, Dolphins and Porpoises.* Richmond Hill, ON: Firefly Books, 2017.

Leiren-Young, Mark. *The Killer Whale Who Changed the World.* Vancouver, BC: Greystone Books, 2016.

Morton, Alexandra. *Listening to Whales.* New York, NY: Ballantine Books, 2002.

———. *In the Company of Whales.* Victoria, BC: Orca Book Publishers, 1993.

Neiwert, David. *Of Orcas and Men: What Killer Whales Can Teach Us.* New York, NY: Overlook Press, 2015.

Rothenberg, David. *Thousand-Mile Song: Whale Music in a Sea of Sound.* New York, NY: Basic Books, 2010.

ACKNOWLEDGMENTS

Some people get involved with environmental issues because they want to save the whales or the forests. I wanted to save the Ogopogo—a mysterious "monster" some people believe lives in Okanagan Lake in British Columbia. When I was in eighth-grade science class in Vancouver, I saw a news story about chemicals being used to kill weeds in the lake, and I thought, This is going to kill the Ogopogo.

My mom suggested we visit the Society Promoting Environmental Conservation (SPEC)—an environmental group fighting to stop the pesticides from being used. The poor woman at SPEC spent about half an hour answering my questions about pesticides. We never talked about the Ogopogo. I got an A on my science project.

The next year, when I was writing about Sasquatch, Mom suggested I call John Green, a guy who wrote a lot of Sasquatch books. This was back when people answered their phones, because the only way to find out who was on the other end of the line was to pick it up.

So this book—and my whole career—started when my mom told me that if I wanted to find out something, I should ask an expert. Thanks, Mom.

Today you can track down almost anyone online. And most people have email.

If you've got a question for someone—including me—never be afraid to ask. Not everyone will answer—although I promise I'll try—but you never know who will.

When I work with researchers, I usually ask for help when answers might take days or weeks to find on my own. For this book I was lucky enough to get help from several amazing researchers, including Lily Campbell, Emma Eslake, Chantelle Huard and Carden Serviss. These awesome women also helped double-check my facts.

That doesn't mean there might not be new—or more accurate—information by the time you read this book. We find out new things about orcas and our world every day. If there are any interesting updates in orca world—or if I've made any mistakes—I'll share them online at orcaseverywhere.com.

I'd also like to thank the orca experts from around the world who welcomed me into their pod—especially the experts who've always been happy to answer my questions: Ken Balcomb (founder of the Center for Whale Research in Washington State), Lance Barrett-Lennard (director of the Marine Mammal Research Program at the Vancouver Aquarium), author and research pioneer John Ford, Howard Garrett (Orca Network), acoustic expert Kristen Jasper Kanes, Jeffery Ventre (co-founder of the advocacy group Voice of the Orcas), Lori Marino (president of the Whale Sanctuary Project) and Alexandra Morton (orca and salmon researcher and author of the first orca books published by Orca).

Historian Jason Colby shared his insights, ideas and research with me. He also loaned me his ace researcher, Isobel Griffin, to help answer my questions.

Thanks to my early readers like Ann Eriksson for comments and notes.

I have some fantastic friends, including Joan Watterson and Darron Leiren-Young, who started this wild Moby ride with me. Ian and Will Ferguson loaned me a place in Calgary—and pretty much locked me up there—to write my first draft.

Thanks to all the people who shared their photos here, including the men who were part of the Moby Doll story: Joe Bauer, Murray Newman, Pat McGeer and Terry McLeod.

I received information and art from Sirún Almeida from Whales of Iceland; Jody White, collection manager at the Eden Killer Whale Museum in Australia; Dawn Noren, research fishery biologist at the National Oceanic and Atmospheric Administration (NOAA); and Greg McKee, director of the documentary *Killers of Eden*, about Old Tom.

This book wouldn't exist if Yvonne Gall hadn't commissioned and produced my radio documentary about Moby Doll, *The Killer Whale That Changed the World*, for CBC's *Ideas*.

It also wouldn't exist if Rob Sanders at Greystone Books hadn't asked me to write a book about Moby Doll and editor Nancy Flight hadn't helped me turn that idea into *The Killer Whale Who Changed the World*. Everyone I thanked for helping me with that book also deserves thanks here, because it provided much of the information for this one (and gave Orca Books associate publisher Ruth Linka the idea that I might be able to write a book like this).

It was a treat to have editor Sarah Harvey take me into the world of writing for readers like you. Jenn Playford brought the look of the book to life, Jen Cameron and the marketing team took the book out into the world, and the rest of the Orca pod helped make sure this was the best book it could possibly be.

I'm delighted to thank the team at the Royal BC Museum, especially Gavin Hanke (the museum's curator of vertebrate zoology), who shared their orca ideas with me and invited me to work with them to bring their fantastic orca exhibit to the world.

And, finally, thanks to the always-awesome Rayne Ellycrys Benu, who took some of the photos in the book and who watches the whales with me as we try to share their stories to help save their pods and their home.

INDEX

*Page numbers in **bold** indicate an image caption.*

MORE FROM THE
ORCA WILD SERIES

ORCA WILD

ACT FOR THE WILD BEFORE IT'S TOO LATE!

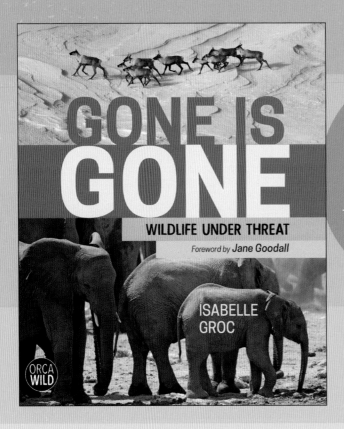

GONE IS GONE

WILDLIFE UNDER THREAT

Foreword by *Jane Goodall*

ISABELLE GROC

ORCA WILD

"Everyone should read this book. And I mean everyone."

—Virginia McKenna, co-founder, Born Free Foundation

Learn about why species become endangered, how scientists are learning about endangered wildlife, what people are doing to conserve species and ways young people can help.

READ THE WILD.
SAVE THE WILD.

ORCA